~ Deviled Eggs ~
~ Shells In The Yolk ~

By Olivia Valency

ISBN: 979-8-9946200-7-6

Any mention of Calvinism is specific to the church where I grew up and how I recall it being taught to me by my mom, teachers, and preachers throughout my life. It's not always taught the same way in all Calvinist churches. All quoted scripture is from the King James Version Bible unless noted otherwise.

Some names, locations, and dates are changed for privacy reasons.

First edition, March 2026

Books written by Olivia Valency

Scrambled Eggs ~ Walking on Shells

Sunny Side Up ~ Eggshells to Seashells

Deviled Eggs ~ Shells in the Yolk

Poached Eggs ~ Selling Empty Shells

Over Easy ~ Cracking the Shell

Special thanks to my daughters,
Hannah and Heather,
for proofreading and editing.

TABLE OF CONTENTS

~ Broken Wings ~

When my daughter Hannah graduated from high school, I planned and organized a graduation party for her. I invited Mom, my siblings, and their spouses and children. My family is enormous. To ensure we had enough space, I rented the private school gymnasium where we all attended school.

After I became an adult, I occasionally organized family get-togethers with my extended family. Our family experienced tremendous trauma and abuse during childhood. My brothers and sisters, in different ways, all became quite dysfunctional. Most of the time, everyone attended these family events. Most people also showed up that day.

My husband and I were having marital problems again. This time, we had moved into separate homes. After enduring his abuse for twenty years, I was now considering divorce. Even though we were dealing with serious personal issues, we made the trip together.

I told Mom what I was going through. I asked her to keep it private and not share it with anyone else. That didn't work out so well. Asking a gossiper not to gossip is like asking a bird not to poop. She sang like a canary and shared my situation with my sisters.

As everyone arrived and settled in, my sister Danielle approached me. She asked to talk to me. I said, "Sure, what's up?" She asked if we could speak privately in the school bathroom. What on earth could be so important that it needed such privacy?

Once we entered the bathroom, Danielle said she had heard about my getting a divorce. I guess a little birdie must have told her? As crazy as a coot, trying to save my soul from hell, she began attacking me. She said that divorce is wrong, and God requires me to make my marriage work — no matter what. She said God would permit divorce if someone committed an act of physical adultery.

I had to wing it as Danielle barged into my personal life. Her attacks were unexpected and uninvited. She caught me off guard. My head started spinning as I realized she didn't just know about my business, but she was attempting to feather my nest. Meanwhile, I had to process that Mom had just betrayed me. My heart sank into my stomach. I felt nauseous and in need of a sick bucket.

My voice sounded weak as I explained to her the abuse I had been enduring for twenty years. As tears filled my eyes, I told her how much I was hurting. I couldn't take all of his lies, stealing, and pornography anymore. The Bible says lusting after other women is committing adultery. I saw him as cheating on me.

Danielle wouldn't listen to the pain in my heart. She wanted to take me under her wing and teach me her beliefs. Her primary goal was to warn me about the consequences of divorce.

She wasn't there to be a friend or to offer comfort. Instead, she was there to preach against the "sin" I was about to commit. Her advice felt intrusive and judgmental. She demanded that I feather my nest her way, as she believes her nest is feathered better than mine.

Danielle pecked at me for thirty minutes. I became annoyed and told her I needed to do what was right for myself. I told her that our Heavenly Father doesn't want me to remain with an abuser. He desires me to be happy. Danielle kept pressuring me. To make her stop, I asked her to mind her own business. I reiterated that I had to do what made me happy.

Danielle wouldn't stop ruffling my feathers. She was desperate. She wanted to rule my roost! My anger grew, and my skin began to tingle. I said again, more firmly, for her to stay out of it! As I started walking away from her, she snidely said, "Well, I'll pray for you!" I was at my wits' end with her poking her eagle eye into my affairs. She was trampling on my damaged heart and now giving me haughty prayers.

I was steaming now. Danielle's pompous attitude offended me. Her condescending religious hierarchy was oozing from her peacock feathers. My jaw hit the floor. My eyes opened wide. Becoming angry, I yelled, "That's judging!" I walked away. I didn't want her prayers. All I needed was a friend to love me and comfort my injured heart.

Danielle went crying to our siblings. Devastated that I had shouted at her, she played the victim. She portrayed me as being at fault for her attacking me with her judgments. After meddling in my affairs, she turned me into a dirty bird. After dumping her bird turd on me, Danielle then took her religious feathers and flew the coop. She didn't even say goodbye to me or my family.

Feeling overwhelmed with sadness, I struggled to carry on with the party. I pretended nothing had happened and that I was fine. I was far from okay. Because of Danielle's mistaken religious beliefs — believing that hammers are used to save souls from hell — she killed two birds with one stone. She destroyed our relationship that day, took my injured heart, stomped on it, and shattered it into a million pieces.

After a year of emotional healing, I reached out to Danielle to see if we could mend our relationship. I said, "Hey, we're sisters. Things shouldn't be like this." I told her I was sorry for getting angry at her. She responded, "Well, you told me to mind my own business!"

With a slight chuckle, I said, "If we had that exact discussion today, I'd still ask you to mind your own business, but I wouldn't get angry like I did."

She haughtily quipped, "Well, that's the way it is then." She wouldn't forgive me unless I apologized for telling her to stay out of my affairs.

I said, "Okay. Well, I love you." It was an awkward goodbye. She didn't want to fix our relationship. Things would stay distant and aloof between us. Boy, oh boy, was I ever right! Danielle and I haven't spoken in 13 years!

Suppose I told Danielle I had no right. Would things have been different? I don't think so. She would still condemn me, as she suffers from a religious hierarchy. She believes everyone who isn't a member of her "God's only truth" church is a gentile destined for hell.

Danielle's church taught her to save sinners by barging into their personal lives and to admonish them with God's sledgehammer. She is to confront them about their sins and shame them into submission. If they don't listen, she is to shake the dust off her feet and abandon them. Devastation struck our entire family that day.

Her words cut deep and reminded me of the past pain caused by our dad. However, he threw actual physical hammers at us. Hammers break wings, and make it so people can no longer fly.

Attacking me at my daughter's party? Who does that? It was a day for celebration! What did she expect would happen? She may have thought I would say, "Oh, Danielle, you're so right! I'll remain with this liar, thief, and adulterer! I'll live my life in misery because you say that's what your God requires of me. Shame on me for even thinking about a divorce. Please forgive me for my sinful thoughts. I promise I'll obey your religious rules from now on so I don't go to hell."

I do not want Danielle's telephone to heaven. She should pray for herself. I have my own phone to heaven. My Poppa is my friend and my comforter. I love Him, and He loves me. I'm sure he feels upset with Danielle for poking me with her judgment stick.

Our family fell apart after this tragic incident. All the effort I put into planning parties and trying to keep our fragile, broken family united in love came crashing down that day. I tell you, with many tears still flowing, Danielle destroyed our family with one fell swoop of her tongue. She shattered the fragile string that was holding us together. She has a lot to apologize for.

I hope someday Father will show Danielle the pain her actions have caused, and we can find healing. I long for the day she offers me an apology. Then we can be sisters again. We will love each other and live together forever in heaven.

Suppose Danielle doesn't apologize to me in this lifetime. In that case, I'm 100% sure she'll feel humiliated and embarrassed when she faces Jesus. I'm 99.9% sure I'll receive an apology from her then. I'll forgive her, of course.

I understand this is Satan's world. Because he has brainwashed Danielle, she believes she shouldn't give love and comfort to me. She believes Satan's lies. She thinks she's supposed to reprimand others. If they won't listen to her admonitions or accept her doctrine, she's told to stop associating with them. Her church tells her to dump them like a hot potato and mark them as hell-bound.

Wow! If Jesus acted that way, nobody would ever go to heaven! Isaiah 64:6 says, "All our righteousnesses are as filthy rags." We all need His cleansing and forgiveness. We can't carry the thorns of judgment and the thistles of criticism to help others. Instead, we are to show love, compassion, and understanding. We should help people rather than hurt them. That's what Jesus and His servants do.

This wasn't the first time Danielle had hurt me. As a teenager, I admitted myself to the hospital because of an eating disorder. I had experienced a few major losses as a young child and had seen my older sisters endure violent abuse.

Some of my siblings called me hurtful names. Some kids at school also called me names and would stick their feet out to trip me when I walked past their desks. I was never taught how to love myself or stand up for myself. My stomach was tight, and I always felt anxious and on high alert.

After I got out of the hospital, I was lying on my bed. Guess who knocked on my bedroom door? Yep, you guessed right! Danielle knocked and asked, "Can I talk to you about something?" (No wonder I felt like I needed the sick bucket when she said those exact words at the party.) I'm still traumatized to this day.

She had her nose high in the air and a haughty look on her face. She didn't ask me how I was doing or if she could help. Nope, her words cut into my heart like a hot knife through butter. She said, "I used to look up to you. I don't anymore. I disrespect you now because of this."

I felt shocked as she exuded an air of high excellence. My heart exploded with extreme sadness. Wow! I needed love and comfort. During my time of needing a friend, Danielle showed me she was neither my sister nor my friend. We weren't especially close as sisters, but we also weren't enemies. After she left, my tears flowed like a river — very long and very hard.

I realized I had nobody who loved or cared about me. If I were to survive, I needed to follow what they told me at the hospital. They said it was crucial for me to love myself, to be assertive, and to stand up for myself. I understood that no one else would give me the love I needed, so I had to do it myself. My tears eased as I curled up in the fetal position on my bed. I started thinking about how to do this.

Looking back, I wonder if Danielle hadn't been so cruel to me that day; if she hadn't shattered my already bruised and wounded heart, would I have started down my path of self-love and assertiveness? Hmmm. Maybe not. I suppose I owe Danielle a thank you for pushing me to the depths of hell. There was only one way out. Self-love was the answer. Our relationship became strained after this incident. After we both married, we treated each other with respect — right until the day she decided not to anymore.

~ Cooked Goose ~

After Danielle's abandonment, I found comfort and wisdom in the Bible. It helped me recover from Danielle's woodpecker-induced trauma. Our Poppa has given us valuable advice and important lessons. He has made it easy to get a bird's-eye view of how He requires us to love and forgive others:

"And the mean man shall be brought down, and the mighty man shall be humbled, and the eyes of the lofty shall be humbled" (Isa 5:15).

Danielle doesn't see herself as mean or lofty. Still, whenever we judge and criticize others, we are not being kind and humble.

"Blessed are the peacemakers: for they shall be called the children of God" (Mt 5:9).

Judging, criticizing, and meddling in people's affairs cause conflict and division. This is not being a peacemaker. Peaceful people are children of God.

"And above all things have fervent charity among yourselves: for charity shall cover the multitude of sins" (1 Pet 4:8).

Charity - Strong's G26 - Love, i.e., affection or benevolence, a love-feast, charity(-ably), dear, love. Strong's H160 - 1) Brotherly love, affection, goodwill, love, benevolence. 2) Love feasts. In this context, charity means love, reminding us that love covers a multitude of faults.

"And the servant of the Lord must not strive; but be gentle unto all men, apt to teach, patient. In meekness instructing those that oppose themselves" (2 Tim 2:24-25).

We must be gentle, patient, and loving to others. Instructing with meekness means offering helpful options or solutions they can try, but only when they ask for advice. We should not interfere in others' affairs unless invited to share our opinion. People are more receptive to kind, caring, loving, and encouraging words.

We can attract more flies with honey. The fly swatter causes strife. A meek person refrains from intruding on others' lives and refrains from judging them. Meekness means being compassionate and offering support, understanding that we all make mistakes. A self-righteous hypocrite acts as if they have no sin. They think their sins are better than others'. They ignore their own sins and believe they are doing God's work when they barge in uninvited to point out our faults.

"This is my commandment, That ye love one another, as I have loved you. Greater love hath no man than this, that a man lay down his life for his friends" (Jn 15:12-13).

The reason Danielle didn't show me proper love is that she doesn't understand how much our Father loves us both. Poppa, please show Danielle how much you love her so she can know how she is supposed to love me. Poppa loves us so much that He laid down His life to die for us. He paid our debt for our disobedience and rebellion.

"And walk in love, as Christ also hath loved us … Ye are my friends, if ye do whatsoever I command you" (Eph 5:2, 14).

We are Jesus' friends if we do everything He says — including loving one another. Hitting people with hellfire, damnation, and judgment hammers isn't loving one another. That's not meek, edifying, comforting, supportive, or gentle. Love is the answer. We must be kind, always sharing our Father's love with others.

"Be ye angry, and sin not: let not the sun go down upon your wrath: … Let no corrupt communication proceed out of your mouth, but that which is good to the use of edifying, that it may minister grace unto the hearers. … Let all bitterness, and wrath, and anger, and clamour, and evil speaking, be put away from you, with all malice" (Eph 4:26, 29, 31).

I still feel some righteous indignation toward Danielle for meddling in my personal matters. Father said only a fool would pull on a dog's ears. If we poke at someone who is hurting or meddle in their affairs, we're bound to get bitten. If we're compassionate, kind, and supportive, love will flourish.

Sisters should be friends. Danielle was supposed to uplift me and show love through kindness and understanding. It was her job to comfort me and care for my wounds during my deep trauma. Instead, she tore me down. Her communication was corrupt. Danielle became bitter toward me and has since treated me as if I were her enemy.

"But I say unto you, That whosoever is angry with his brother without a cause shall be in danger of the judgment: … Therefore if thou bring thy gift to the altar … first be reconciled to thy brother, and then come and offer thy gift. And be ye kind one to another, tenderhearted, forgiving one another, even as God for Christ's sake hath forgiven you" (Matthew 5:22-24, 32).

Danielle got mad at me. She believes I should apologize, even though she started it. Her church told her to go out goose hunting and shoot down as many honky tonkers as possible. However, if we don't love others, our goose is gonna get cooked.

Father doesn't accept our gifts to Him until we first make things right with our brothers and sisters. Either we are acting lovingly, or we are acting hatefully. There's no in-between; no gray area; and no heaven for a half-hateful person.

Poppa forgives us when we tell Him we are sorry. He expects us to forgive others. The following story shows us that Poppa gets upset with us if we don't forgive others:

> Therefore is the kingdom of heaven likened unto a certain king, which would take account of his servants. And when he had begun to reckon, one was brought unto him, which owed him ten thousand talents. But forasmuch as he had not to pay, his lord commanded him to be sold, and his wife, and children, and all that he had, and payment to be made. The servant therefore fell down, and worshipped him, saying, Lord, have patience with me, and I will pay thee all. Then the lord of that

> servant was moved with compassion, and loosed him, and forgave him the debt.
>
> But the same servant went out, and found one of his fellow servants, which owed him an hundred pence: and he laid hands on him, and took him by the throat, saying, Pay me that thou owest. And his fellow servant fell down at his feet, and besought him, saying, Have patience with me, and I will pay thee all. And he would not, but went and cast him into prison, till he should pay the debt. So when his fellow servants saw what was done, they were very sorry, and came and told unto their lord all that was done.
>
> Then his lord, after that he had called him, said unto him, O thou wicked servant, I forgave thee all that debt, because thou desiredst me: Shouldest not thou also have had compassion on thy fellow servant, even as I had pity on thee? And his lord was wroth, and delivered him to the tormentors, till he should pay all that was due unto him. So likewise shall my heavenly Father do also unto you, if ye from your hearts forgive not every one his brother their trespasses. (Mt 18:23-35)

Father has a day of reckoning for all His servants. Everyone will have their day in court to face the King. We can't fly the coop on that day. When the hammer hits the gavel, the Judge will declare each person either guilty or not guilty.

Years before she broke my wings, Danielle had cried out to the King, asking to be saved from punishment. She had repented to our Poppa for the previous debt she owed Him. The King had forgiven Danielle for all her debts. Jesus paid the price for all of us when we repent. Every parent's heart melts with forgiveness when their child cries out with heartfelt sorrow for their misbehavior. Our Poppa is the same.

After the King forgave Danielle her sins, she came after me, one of her fellow servants. Searching me out, she shoved my perceived sin debt into my face. She threatened me with eternal damnation. She did all this in the name of the compassionate King, who had just forgiven her massive debt to Him.

Now, she has this new debt in the Heavenly Books under her name. It will stay there until she tells me she is sorry. She is required to settle her debt before entering heaven.

Sincere apologies make Father use His forgiveness eraser. Repentance removes the wrongdoings recorded in heaven.

The tormentors described in the story take many forms. Some believe it's karma when they see someone getting their goose cooked. Father does or allows punishment and suffering based on what each person deserves. He uses whatever discipline is necessary to bring each child to rock bottom. He wants us to look up and choose His path of love.

Father is just and fair. He is also compassionate and loving. He forgives us when we apologize. We must do the same to others.

"We know that we have passed from death unto life, because we love the brethren. He that loveth not his brother abideth in death. Whosoever hateth his brother is a murderer: and ye know that no murderer hath eternal life abiding in him" (1 Jn 3:14-15).

Father considers us murderers if we hate others. Hurtful words and actions leave lasting adverse psychological effects. Hate makes people feel sad and steals their joy. When we love others, we know we have passed into eternal life.

"Touch not mine anointed, and do my prophets no harm" (Ps 105:15).

"It is impossible but that offences will come: but woe unto him, through whom they come! It were better for him that a millstone were hanged about his neck, and he cast into the sea, than that he should offend one of these little ones … If thy brother trespass against thee, rebuke him; and if he repent, forgive him" (Lu 17:1-3).

People will hurt us, but woe to those who do. Poppa has a big stick! It's better for these people if they drown in the sea than to hurt one of Father's little ones. When Poppa pulls out His paddle, they'll be screaming, "Code Brown! Code Brown!" as the goose poop hits the fan.

If we are cruel to one of His little ones, Father has a spanking paddle of sorts. He will give us specific lessons to help us become more humble, kind, and loving. Many people don't realize when they are experiencing Poppa's paddle. They blame their misfortune on bad luck.

We should rebuke people only if they are hurtful to us. If they apologize, Father says to forgive them. If they don't, then forgiveness isn't required. For our own peace of mind, it's better to forgive them in our hearts. Feel sorry for them, as they haven't learned to love themselves. Those who love themselves will also show love to others.

The conflict started because I was contemplating a divorce. How would Danielle react if she found out that Father had gotten divorced? His divorce doesn't fit her strict, mistaken belief. She thinks physical adultery is the only acceptable reason for divorce.

"And I saw, when for all the causes whereby backsliding Israel committed adultery I had put her away, and given her a bill of divorce yet her treacherous sister Judah feared not, but went and played the harlot also" (Jer 3:8).

Father's definition of adultery differs from Danielle's. Father divorced the ten tribes of Israel because they had committed adultery in their hearts. They were chasing after, lusting after, and worshipping other gods. Danielle's church portrays divorce as the ultimate transgression. They'd likely judge and condemn Poppa, making Him sit at the back of the church.

"Ye have heard that it was said by them of old time, Thou shalt not commit adultery: But I say unto you, That whosoever looketh on a woman to lust after her hath committed adultery with her already in his heart" (Mt 5:27-28).

My husband was lusting after other women in his heart. I had every biblical right to divorce.

"Saul, Saul, why persecutest thou me? … And I said, Who art thou, Lord? And he said, I am Jesus whom thou persecutest" (Acts 26:14-15).

Saul was a deeply religious man. He believed he was serving God by arresting and executing Christians. Danielle is also a very religious woman. She thinks she is serving God by chastising sinners. She is the new sheriff in town.

If we attack Christians, it is a direct attack on Jesus. Those who love Jesus are the body of Christ.

"And the King shall answer and say unto them, Verily I say unto you, Inasmuch as ye have done it unto one of the least of these my brethren, ye have done it unto me … Inasmuch as ye did it not to one of the least of these, ye did it not to me" (Mt 25:40, 45).

"He shall not cry, nor lift up, nor cause his voice to be heard in the street. A bruised reed shall he not break" (Is 42:2, 3).

Jesus is not a loud, condescending bully who yells at people on street corners. Jesus is soft-spoken, gentle, and peaceful. He catches flies with honey. I was a bruised reed. Jesus would have offered me comfort and compassion. Jesus doesn't break bruised reeds.

~ Wild Goose Chase ~

Everyone is on a learning journey — their own wild goose chase of sorts. Everyone makes mistakes. They help us learn what is good, bad, right, and wrong. We aren't born perfect. We didn't come with an instruction manual. Thank you, Poppa, for being so loving, patient, and forgiving toward us — your really messy children.

"Judge not, that ye be not judged. For with what judgment ye judge, ye shall be judged: … Or how wilt thou say to thy brother, Let me pull out the mote out of thine eye; and, behold, a beam is in thine own eye? Thou hypocrite, first cast out the beam out of thine own eye; and then shalt thou see clearly to cast out the mote out of thy brother's eye" (Mt 7:1-5).

Like poop through a goose — we all receive the same judgment we give others.

Jesus said not to meddle in other people's matters. If we judge others, they'll judge us. They'll point out our faults, saying, "How can you judge me when you have your own sins?" The scribes and Pharisees who crucified Jesus loved to goose up and act holier-than-thou. We all sin and fall short of perfection in different ways.

Treat others the way we want to be treated. If we bite, judge, or criticize others, they will bite back. Such behavior damages relationships and families.

A mote is a tiny fragment or piece of sawdust. A beam is a large 2 x 12 piece of wood. Why should we concern ourselves with other people's sins as if theirs are worse? We are all in the same boat. Instead of being enemies, we must support and uplift each other. Together, we are to block the temptations that Satan is throwing at us.

"For whosoever shall keep the whole law, and yet offend in one point he is guilty of all" (Jas 2:10).

"Therefore thou art inexcusable, O man, whosoever thou art that judgest: for wherein thou judgest another, thou condemnest thyself; for thou that judgest doest the same things" (Rom 2:1).

If we break even one of Father's rules, we break the entire set. The person who breaks the rule against bearing false witness is no better than someone who breaks the adultery rule. Both are equally guilty.

The Ten Commandments don't mention divorce. Instead, they say, "Thou shalt not bear false witness." Everyone who gossips is likely violating this commandment. Most gossip contains half-truths. Even if the gossip is 1% false, it still falls under Father's rule.

"And thinkest thou this, O man, that judgest them which do such things, and doest the same, that thou shalt escape the judgment of God?" (Rom 2:3).

Don't count your chickens before they hatch. Nobody can avoid their court hearing. Everyone will face their Heavenly Father as He sits on His judgment seat. Poppa knows the whole truth about everything. He will bring everything into the light. Everyone will receive punishment or rewards based on what they deserve. I'm aiming for many rewards. Our Poppa owns everything. To receive His vast inheritance, we must choose love. Evil and unloving people will receive indignation and wrath — nothing but a big ol' goose egg.

"Or despisest thou the riches of his goodness and forbearance and longsuffering; not knowing that the goodness of God leadeth thee to repentance?" (Rom 2:4).

We are to teach others about Poppa's goodness and how much He loves us. That will inspire them to love and please Him in return. When we have Father's Spirit within us, we strive to care for others the way He cares for us. We must leave judgment in His hands. Sharing His love is our job.

"But after thy hardness and impenitent heart treasurest up unto thyself wrath against the day of wrath and revelation of the righteous judgment of God; Who will render to every man according to his deeds" (Rom 2:5, 6).

Hardhearted individuals don't feel remorse for breaking His rules. They don't apologize when they are unkind to others. They are tough birds that ultimately need to be cooked a bit. Father will cook their goose. He will reveal everything, and His judgment will be fair and correct.

At any moment, we can ask forgiveness of Poppa and others. Otherwise, we can address those rebellions and hurts when

Jesus arrives on earth. I'd prefer to settle it beforehand. With a clean slate, I can run and jump into His arms. I'll want at least a thousand hugs from Him on the first day.

If we delay apologies until Jesus returns, our faces will light up with such joy when we first see Him. But then, as He reminds us of how we treated others, goosebumps will appear all over our bodies. Our faces will fall into ashamed and fearful expressions. We fell for the lies that the wolves in sheep's clothing told us.

The wolves didn't teach to love sinners. Jesus ate with sinners. He showed them love and forgiveness. Unfortunately, those wolves taught that Jesus loves us only if we're members of a specific church. They misled people into thinking that all of their geese are swans. The only membership that matters is entrance into heaven, and that has nothing to do with a church building.

Father's servants plant seeds of His love to others. It is our job to teach people about heaven. Our Father wants all His children to choose love.

"To them who by patient continuance in well doing seek for glory and honour and immortality, eternal life" (Rom 2:7).

The goose hangs high for us who focus on buying our eternal life insurance policy. We strive patiently to do good and to please Father. Our reward will be to have eternal life with Him. Heaven offers unimaginable peace, joy, love, and happiness. I long for that day. I'm also looking forward to receiving my rewards.

"But unto them that are contentious, and don't obey the truth, but obey unrighteousness, indignation and wrath, Tribulation and anguish, upon every soul of man that doeth evil" (Rom 2:8, 9).

Contentious people cause conflict, hold grudges, and judge others. Jesus is the Way, the Truth, and the Life. He said to love our Father above all and to love others as we love ourselves.

Danielle believes her sins are nonexistent or less severe than mine. Since she now considers herself perfect, she feels she can teach others. Some people don't see their sins as bad as yours. They justify to themselves why breaking the rules is okay for them.

She doesn't consider sharing other people's matters to be gossip. She justifies her gossip as simply sharing important news. We should mind our own business so we don't get caught up in spreading half-truths.

"But glory, honour, and peace, to every man that worketh good … For there is no respect of persons with God" (Rom 2:10, 11).

We should be patient, understanding, compassionate, loving, gentle, and forgiving to others. That will earn us glory, honor, blessings, rewards, joy, peace, love, and happiness — alongside our Poppa — forever.

It's not a game of Duck, Duck, Goose — Father doesn't favor any child with special treatment. What's good for the goose is good for the gander. A good father disciplines His children when they disobey — it's for their own good. Poppa said no because it's harmful to us or others. Father doesn't create silly rules without a reason. He's a genius — Poppa always knows best!

Those who have "sinned without law shall also perish without law: … sinned in the law shall be judged by the law; … the doers of the law shall be justified … which have not the law, … are a law unto themselves: … law written in their hearts, their conscience also bearing witness, and their thoughts" (Rom 2:12-15).

Judgment for each person will be correct and based on whether we had the Bible — the written law. If not, did we listen to our conscience and gut instinct? Father has embedded His law within us. He gave us an innate sense of good and evil. No one will have any excuse for disobeying their gut instincts and conscience.

Everything is a choice. Our gut and conscience always know the correct answer. It's crucial to listen to the built-in alarm bells. Love is always the answer. Our intuition is that slight prickling that pops up and speaks to us. Always trust your gut. Do the prickles feel loving, or are they warning you that something is a bit off and doesn't feel quite right?

"In the day when God shall judge the secrets of men by Jesus Christ according to my gospel" (Rom 2:16).

There are no secrets. Father will reveal everything. Who can stand before Him without feeling embarrassment and shame? Only we who love Poppa — those of us who have turned our lives around to follow Him.

"Thou therefore which teachest another, teachest thou not thyself? thou that preachest a man should not steal, dost thou steal? Thou that sayest a man should not commit adultery, dost thou commit adultery? thou that abhorrest idols, dost thou commit sacrilege?" (Rom 2:21, 22).

Christians have specific instructions in His letter about how to behave. Religious hypocrites think it's religious to preach His rules. All the while, they haven't trained themselves to obey them perfectly. They focus on other people's mistakes, even though they share the same guilt. Let's get our own ducks in a row. Then, we can go to other people's ponds to straighten out their ducks.

Show me one person who doesn't break Father's rules. Then, I'll show you someone who doesn't need Jesus' sacrificial gift. We can embrace Jesus' gift, or we can suffer our own punishments.

Everyone can enter heaven if we ask for forgiveness and love Him. It's not a wild-goose chase. All Father wants is our love and that we obey His rules. Poppa warned not to follow Satan's destructive, vulgar, and harmful ways. Give a wholehearted effort to loving and serving Him. He is the King of Kings, the Master Magician, and the owner of the universe.

~ Muckety Ducks ~

We must obey Father's rules. None of us can follow them perfectly, so it's best to focus on our own path and let others focus on theirs. We are all on a journey, each trying to do our best. We have all broken Father's rules, and He loves us all equally.

"Speak not evil one of another, brethren. He that speaketh evil of his brother, and judgeth his brother, speaketh evil of the law, and judgeth the law: but if thou judge the law, thou art not a doer of the law, but a judge. There is one lawgiver, who is able to save and to destroy: who art thou that judgest another? Therefore to him that knoweth to do good, and doeth it not, to him it is sin" (Jas 4:11-12, 17).

It's not our place to judge others. Father is the judge. Only He can see into our minds. Our role is to love and show kindness. Knowing that we are not to judge, choosing the opposite is a sin.

"A new commandment I give unto you, That ye love one another; as I have loved you, that ye also love one another. By this shall all men know that ye are my disciples, if ye have love one to another" (Jn 13:34, 35).

Father's servants will love and be compassionate to everyone.

"But he that is greatest among you shall be your servant. And whosoever shall exalt himself shall be abased; and he that shall humble himself shall be exalted" (Mt 23:11,12).

Father's servants serve love to everyone. We listen with compassion and understanding. Patience and kindness make all the difference. Love is the honey that catches the flies. In Father's eyes, the greatest are those who serve His love.

If we have a muckety-duck attitude, criticizing, judging, and attacking others, Father will abase us. His servants are humble and serve with patience and peace. They don't exalt themselves or shame others. We share how amazing He is and what Jesus did for us.

"If ye love me, keep my commandments … He that hath my commandments, and keepeth them, he it is that loveth me: and he that loveth me shall be loved of my Father, and I will love him, and will manifest myself to him" (Jn 14:15, 21).

Nobody can earn eternal life by perfectly obeying His two main commandments. Everyone makes mistakes. We can suffer our punishment. However, Jesus paid our debt. He offers a much less painful way for us to be washed clean.

Only those who are clean can enter heaven. Jesus can wash away our filth. To enter heaven, we must ask forgiveness and love Him. Easy Cheesy!

Since a wild goose never lays a tame egg, those who follow Satan choose hate. We need Father to help us defend against his fiery darts and deceptions. We need Jesus as our protector. With Him in us, we have power over all our enemies. Our enemy is Satan, who wants our souls to perish along with his own.

Satan hates Father. The way he harms Poppa is by corrupting His children. It's a spiritual war — a battle between good and evil. Father allows Satan to dump his evil among us. Poppa is testing and proving us. He is culling out all the dirty birds. Only those who embrace love and kindness will enter heaven.

The following Bible story shows us that love for Father, love for ourselves, and love for others are exactly what allow us into heaven:

> And, behold, a certain lawyer stood up, and tempted him, saying, Master, what shall I do to inherit eternal life? He said unto him, What is written in the law? how readest thou? And he answering said, Thou shalt love the Lord thy God with all thy heart, and with all thy soul, and with all thy strength, and with all thy mind; and thy neighbour as thyself. And he said unto him, Thou hast answered right: this do, and thou shalt live.
>
> But he, willing to justify himself, said unto Jesus, And who is my neighbour? And Jesus answering said, A certain man went down from Jerusalem to Jericho, and fell among thieves, which stripped him of his raiment, and wounded him, and departed, leaving him half dead. And by chance there came down a certain priest that way: and when he saw him,

> he passed by on the other side. And likewise a Levite, when he was at the place, came and looked on him, and passed by on the other side.
>
> But a certain Samaritan, as he journeyed, came where he was: and when he saw him, he had compassion on him, And went to him, and bound up his wounds, pouring in oil and wine, and set him on his own beast, and brought him to an inn, and took care of him. And on the morrow when he departed, he took out two pence, and gave them to the host, and said unto him, Take care of him; and whatsoever thou spendest more, when I come again, I will repay thee.
>
> Which now of these three, thinkest thou, was neighbour unto him that fell among the thieves? And he said, He that shewed mercy on him. Then said Jesus unto him, Go, and do thou likewise. (Lu 10:25-37)

The priest and the Levite did not show compassion. Love matters more than religious status. They didn't do what it takes to inherit eternal life. They didn't love their neighbor; they judged him. If a person becomes wounded — they need comfort and care. That's just common sense.

The Good Samaritan — a non-religious person — stopped and helped. If Danielle had been that Good Samaritan, she would have hugged me and held me. She would have said, "I love you, and Father loves you too! He will help you through this. I'm sorry someone did all these bad things to you. I feel your pain. What a bad person it is that shattered your heart like this. How can I help you? I'm here for you, whatever you need. I'll be your friend. I'll never share your business with others. I'm a trustworthy person. How can I comfort you?"

Good Samaritans show compassion. They help wounded people — both physically and emotionally. They don't hit their wounded neighbor with religious hammers.

The nonreligious Good Samaritan will inherit heaven. Only those who love their neighbors can enter heaven. The religious priest and Levite won't enter heaven. They were too religious and too holy to help and comfort the wounded man in his time of need.

My heart was so wounded. I needed a Good Samaritan to come into my life. My sister didn't just walk past me. Nope, as I lay there on the ground, wounded and half dead, she came over and stomped on me. She crushed my wounded heart into a hundred more pieces than it already was.

~ Peaceful Doves ~

Father's servants teach that the kingdom of heaven is at hand. This means that, because of what Jesus did, access to heaven is now in the palm of our hand. It's readily available to us. Whether people choose this wonderful place isn't our concern. There's no need to get upset about their choices. You do you, and I'll do me.

"And as ye go, preach, saying, The kingdom of heaven is at hand. And whosoever shall not receive you, nor hear your words, when ye depart out of that house or city, shake off the dust of your feet. Behold, I send you forth as sheep in the midst of wolves: be ye therefore wise as serpents, and harmless as doves" (Mt 10:7, 14, 16).

"Shake the dust off your feet" means it's no skin off our nose whether people choose to accept Jesus. Just move on to the next person. We should remain as peaceful as doves — even when people don't want to hear about Jesus or how to attain eternal life.

Jesus didn't say to argue, rebuke, criticize, or force our religious beliefs on others. He didn't say to abandon them and never talk to them again. This approach wouldn't make sense. In the future, they may become more receptive to hearing about Father's love. If we mistreat them, it will push them away.

Jesus sent out His disciples as peaceful doves. He said to preach that salvation is now easily available because of what He did for us. Anyone can accept His gift. We can all have our sins paid for. Just love Father and follow His rules to the best of our ability.

"Be kindly affectioned one to another with brotherly love; in honour preferring one another; Rejoice with them that do rejoice, and weep with them that weep. If it be possible, as much as lieth in you, live peaceably with all men" (Rom 12:10, 15, 18).

We should value others and offer comfort to those who suffer. We should weep with those who weep.

"Have no fellowship with the unfruitful works of darkness, but rather reprove them" (Eph 5:11).

Danielle saw my consideration of divorce as engaging in unfruitful works of darkness. She believed she had biblical grounds to reprove me.

To me, dark works include gossiping, talebearing, judging, criticizing, lying, cheating, stealing, lusting, coveting, murder, rape, molestation, burglary, witchcraft, sorcery — which also includes drugs — prideful ego trips, laziness, whoremongering, pornography, sexual immorality, perversion, vulgarity, vulgar music, vulgar shows, idolizing and worshiping material things, worshiping people, worshiping other gods — such as Ishtar — worshiping angels, and anything else not of our Heavenly Father. These behaviors are not allowed in heaven.

Jesus didn't say that a divorced person can't receive forgiveness or enter heaven. He paid the price for all mistakes. The Bible never claims that divorce is a worse sin than gossiping. While divorce ranks high on Danielle's list of reproving, gossiping does not. Standing against the darkness includes standing against gossip.

Reproving the works of darkness means that if people bring their muddy boots into our personal space, we can admonish them. We can ask them to please remove their muddy boots.

Being peaceful like a dove is a gentle approach. You do you, and I'll do me. Don't harm me, and I won't hurt you. We can coexist peacefully. Our Father loves us all. He is the Potter, and we are the clay. He will shape us into a beautiful flowerpot or an ugly toilet, depending on how much correction each of us needs.

Father doesn't want us to worship Him because we fear hell. He simply desires a loving and respectful Poppa-child relationship. He is the Master Magician who made everything. Poppa is the brilliant computer programmer of the universe.

"For thou hast created all things, and for thy pleasure they are and were created" (Rev 4:11).

Father created us for His pleasure. He has no use for those who do not please Him. He said His two main desires are that we love Him and His other children. Those who please

Him will have peace, joy, love, and happiness forever in heaven.

"Saying, The scribes and the Pharisees sit in Moses' seat" (Mt 23:2).

Moses was the lawgiver. These religious hypocrites sat in Moses' seat. They demanded, "Do this, and don't do that!" They insisted that people follow their traditions and their interpretation of the law. Many churches portray that divorced people must sit at the back of the church. But, lo-and-behold, wouldn't ya know, those who gossip and bear false witness get to sit in the front seats.

Father knows His children will stumble. He understands how Satan causes us to stumble and fall. We simply need to ask forgiveness — in Jesus' name — whenever we make a mistake.

If someone wants to try entering heaven by obeying the law, go ahead and try. You will never pass through those Pearly Gates because no one can follow Father's rules without messing up. Jesus is the only way.

Romans 6:23 says, "The wages of sin are death." Jesus has already paid the price for our death penalty. He paid for our consequences if we love Him and follow His set of rules. Since we can't follow Father's rules perfectly, we should never judge or condemn others who can't do it perfectly either. That's just common sense.

My mistakes are no worse than yours. If you look down on me, thinking my mistakes are worse, good luck when you meet our Heavenly Father. It takes doing better than the self-righteous scribes and Pharisees to enter heaven.

"But be not ye called Rabbi: for one is your Master, even Christ; and all ye are brethren" (Mt 23:8).

Don't call any man Rabbi — or Master. Don't call any man Father. There is only one Father. We are not to reverence any man or call him Reverend. Only show reverence to our Father in heaven. He is our Lord, Savior, and Master — Jesus Christ.

The many-membered body of Jesus lives all over the world. We've accepted Jesus into our hearts. In circumcising our hearts, we've severed ourselves from participating in the sins of the world as much as possible. We have no desire to take part in any of Satan's shenanigans. We only want to please our Father and have a Poppa-child relationship with Him.

We keep Him in our hearts and allow Him to lead and guide us. Although we can never achieve perfection, we strive to be perfect. When we mess up, we apologize and seek forgiveness.

"He that judgeth me is the Lord. Therefore judge nothing before the time, until the Lord come, … that no one of you be puffed up for one against another. What will ye? Shall I come unto you with a rod? or in love, and in the spirit of meekness?" (1 Cor 4:4-6, 21).

God is my judge — God is the judge — God will judge. Ironically, this is the meaning of Danielle's name. Puffing up against another person means acting superior to others. Satan is the destroyer. He ruins relationships with his "I'm holier-than-thou" tricks. He tells them to judge and condemn others. Our enemy — Satan — loves to cause derision, division, and strife. Let us unite with Jesus against our enemy.

Would you prefer I come to you with a hellfire and damnation preaching, or would you rather I bring our Father's Spirit of love and meekness? We all prefer people approaching us as peacefully as a dove.

~ Goose on the Loose ~

Some churches teach that physical adultery is the only biblical ground for divorce. Their definition contradicts Jesus' teachings. The Bible states that a husband lusting after other women in his heart is committing adultery. Because of their biblical illiteracy, people cast stones at others who have gotten a divorce or who are contemplating divorce.

They view divorce as an unforgivable sin. However, divorce is not a greater sin than gossiping. Jesus paid the price for divorce, adultery, and gossiping alike. If someone gets a divorce and it was a sin, they can repent and receive forgiveness. Once forgiven, their slate is wiped clean. People should not hold someone's past divorce or adultery against them. Likewise, we should not hold the past sin of gossiping against a repentant, reformed, and forgiven gossiper.

After He forgives us, Jesus doesn't stay upset about it. Proof of this is in the following Bible story:

> And the scribes and Pharisees brought unto him a woman taken in adultery; and when they had set her in the midst, They say unto him, Master, this woman was taken in adultery, in the very act. Now Moses in the law commanded us, that such should be stoned: but what sayest thou? This they said, tempting him, that they might have to accuse him.

> But Jesus stooped down, and with his finger wrote on the ground, as though he heard them not. So when they continued asking him, he lifted up himself, and said unto them, He that is without sin among you, let him first cast a stone at her. And again he stooped down, and wrote on the ground. And they which heard it, being convicted by their own conscience, went out one by one, beginning at the eldest, even unto the last: and Jesus was left alone, and the woman standing in the midst.
>
> When Jesus had lifted up himself, and saw none but the woman, he said unto her, Woman, where are those thine accusers? hath no man condemned thee? She said, No man, Lord. And Jesus said unto her, Neither do I condemn thee: go, and sin no more. (Jn 8:3-11)

Why didn't these stoners bring the man along, too? Why only the woman? It takes two to tango! Shouldn't the goose and the gander get the same treatment?

Jesus was writing all their sins in the dirt. George, you are guilty of bearing false witness through your gossip. Andy, you've been coveting your neighbor's wife. Henry, you're committing adultery every time you lust after another woman. Tom, stealing money from your employer is a sin. John, Father commands you to honor your father and mother. Bill, you worship celebrities and music stars instead of our Heavenly Father.

The woman saw what Jesus had written. She watched each guilty man leave the room as Jesus wrote their sins. By calling Him Lord, she showed her belief that He is our Lord of Lords and King of Kings. Jesus didn't condemn or judge her. He understands that we all make mistakes. He knew she felt sorrow in her heart for being a goose on the loose.

We shouldn't throw stones at others for their sins. Everyone is guilty of sinning. Someone addicted to gossip needs to focus all their energy on stopping the behavior. When we judge and criticize others, we claim to be perfect and free of sin. If we say we're without sin, then we are hypocrites, liars, and suffer from extreme delusion. We become the stoners who cast stones at others.

Many people don't choose the straight and narrow path that leads to heaven. Many are just playing church. They talk the talk but don't walk the walk. Heaven won't welcome people who cast stones of judgment and criticism at others. It will have no tale-bearers or gossipers. Heaven will have no harmful people. That's why it's called Heaven.

Everyone is on their own unique path. We're all experiencing different events, facing various challenges, and enduring traumas. We should never look down on sinners while exuding a religious hierarchy. Instead, we should treat everyone with love, care, gentleness, patience, understanding, compassion, and forgiveness — just as Jesus did.

The scribes and Pharisees saw themselves as too holy to hang out with sinners. We should avoid acting like that. Instead, we are called to share God's love with others. Our goal is to bring as many children as possible onto Father's team of love.

Satan is the top goose on the loose. He's trying to corrupt, demoralize, and destroy all of Father's children. Satan knows his demise; he knows Father has condemned him to be turned to ashes. He will do everything he can to pollute, deceive, and trick Father's children. He wants to collect as many souls as possible — to perish right alongside himself.

We cannot cast stones of criticism at others. We are all equal sinners; we all have shortcomings; and we all mess up. As we travel through Satan's evil world, we can give others a break. We are all guilty, and we all deserve the death penalty.

The scribes and Pharisees despised Jesus. They hated His simple message that, through sincere repentance, we can receive forgiveness. They opposed His teachings about loving God, ourselves, and others. Those nit-pickers became upset by His teaching that no extra rituals, repetitions, long-drawn-out prayers, sacrifices, ceremonies, or made-up traditions were necessary to enter heaven.

Jesus was cutting into their pocketbooks. These dirty scam artists were making money from selling mite-infested, dirty birds on the temple steps as people entered to worship. They tricked the people into believing that they didn't need to bring their best offering for the forgiveness of sins. People were buying dirty doves from the money changers. They deceived the people with this easy money-making scheme, which turned offerings to God into a meaningless tradition.

"By love serve one another. For all the law is fulfilled in one word, even in this; Thou shalt love thy neighbour as thyself. But the fruit of the Spirit is love, joy, peace, longsuffering, gentleness, goodness, faith, meekness, temperance ... If we live in the Spirit, let us also walk in the Spirit" (Gal 5:13, 14, 22-25).

Jesus' gift gives us great freedom. When we commit our lives to Him, it's now easy to repent and be forgiven. However, this doesn't give us the right to be a frivolous goose on the loose, chasing after fleshly desires. Jesus wants us to walk in His Spirit of love toward one another. If we talk the talk, we must walk the walk.

Walking in the Spirit means keeping Jesus at the center of our thoughts and actions. It involves talking with Him and walking alongside Him. When we keep Jesus close as our best friend, we feel ashamed to pursue the lusts of the flesh. We realize He's right here beside us — right here within us — seeing and hearing everything we do and say.

Our spirit tells us to love and be peaceful. Our flesh says to be a goose on the loose. Living in the Spirit means keeping our focus on the spiritual realm. That realm is right beside us — just behind the veil. When the Spirit of God is in us, we will exude love, kindness, gentleness, peace, joy, patience, compassion, understanding, humility, a slow temper, and forgiveness. There's no law against these amazing behaviors.

The Bible teaches us not to seek vain glory by speaking badly about others to boost our own image. We should not envy other people's spiritual gifts or possessions. Each person has a unique gift from our Father. We need to discover our own gift, learn what we excel at, find what we enjoy doing, and then pursue that path.

~ Geese-ipers ~

I found many verses and stories showing that divorce isn't worse than gossiping. It's interesting to see Poppa's feelings about it:

"Thou shalt not go up and down as a talebearer among thy people ... Thou shalt not hate thy brother in thine heart: thou shalt in any wise rebuke thy neighbour, and not suffer sin upon him. Thou shalt not avenge, nor bear any grudge against the children of thy people, but thou shalt love thy neighbour as thyself: I am the Lord" (Lev 19:16-18).

A tale-bearer is a gossip. Father says, "Don't do it."

Some people read this and think they are supposed to rebuke their neighbors. We know that's not the case. That would actually cause strife and division among our neighbors. The Latin Vulgate Bible, of 383 A.D., translates this to say: "Thou shalt not hate thy brother in thy heart: But reprove him openly, lest thou incur sin through him."

What this means is that if your brother wrongs you, confront him openly rather than holding a grudge against him. Address the issue right away; otherwise, it will consume you from the inside. It's a sin against your mental health to harbor anger. This also aligns with the verse that says not to let the sun go down on your wrath.

If we meddle in our neighbor's affairs by telling him how to live, it will only make him angry and resent us. We would cause him to sin. How can he follow the command to love our neighbor if, through our rebuking and criticizing, we make him hate us? I won't go around rebuking anyone. That would lead to conflict and make them hate me. We should avoid vengefulness and holding grudges.

Religious gossipers hope that evil sinners will die. They believe sinners don't deserve life. They view other people's sins as worse than theirs. Their religious hierarchy is so high up they can't even smell their own filth. They speak condescendingly about others, whom they label as evil sinners.

If these religious gossipers would humble themselves and lower their noses, they'd see they are just as guilty of sinning. Heaven has no hierarchy. Heaven has no geese-ipers.

A brief passage in the Psalms shows how wicked these people are:

> Mine enemies speak evil of me, (saying) When shall he die, and his name perish? And if he come to see me, he speaketh vanity: his heart gathereth iniquity to itself; when he goeth abroad, he telleth it. All that hate me whisper together against me: against me do they devise my hurt. An evil disease, say they, cleaveth fast unto him: and now that he lieth he shall rise up no more. Yea, mine own familiar friend, in whom I trusted, which did eat of my bread, hath lifted up his heel against me. (Ps 41:5-9)

Geese-ipers pretend to be your friends. They flatter you to your face to gather goose juice. When they leave, they spread their new juice to others.

If we're obeying the "love your neighbor" commandment, then we should not gossip or whisper about others. Gossiping shows hatred toward others. It suggests that we believe other people's sins are worse than ours.

These religious gossipers say: "He's an evil sinner! He deserves what has happened to him! Let's beat him up with our gossip. Let's kick him hard so he can't get up again!"

Ah, I believed you were my friend. I thought I could trust you. You came to my house, and I gave you food and drink. Ah, you were just pretending so you could get information. Then, when you left, you gossiped about my affairs to others. Lifting your heels against me, you kicked me when I was down. With your gossip, you stabbed me in the back.

"These six things doth the Lord hate: yea, seven are an abomination unto him: A proud look, a lying tongue, and hands that shed innocent blood, An heart that deviseth wicked imaginations, feet that be swift in running to mischief, A false witness that speaketh lies, and he that soweth discord among brethren" (Prov 6:16-19).

A gossiper is a false witness who spreads half-truths. They always add their own opinionated twists of lemon and lime to the story. They are sowing discord among the people. Father detests their behavior.

Father hates seven things. He despises the proud look shown by those who hold their noses in the air and display a superior attitude. He also hates a lying tongue. God abhors hands that shed innocent blood; this includes murderers of all kinds. Gossipers also shed innocent blood with their words.

God despises hearts that plot wickedness. These people are always trying to scam others. He hates feet that are swift to mischief. Mischievous individuals often seek to cause trouble, destruction, and harm to others. Father also hates false witnesses. They tell lies and gossip with partial truths.

Most of all, Father hates those who sow discord. It is an abomination to Him. He is referring to the contentious person who causes strife, gossips, spreads rumors, and always stirs the pot. They try to keep everyone all fired up, in derision, and hating each other.

"A lying tongue hateth those that are afflicted by it; and a flattering mouth worketh ruin" (Prov 26:28). Gossipers hate those they afflict with their evil tongues.

Many people twist the Bible to fit their narrative. The following verses are a perfect example. Paul was very specific, urging us to admonish the busybody gossips, but some don't read it as such:

"Now we command you, brethren, in the name of our Lord Jesus Christ, that ye withdraw yourselves from every brother that walketh disorderly, and not after the tradition which he received of us. For yourselves know how ye ought to follow us: for we behaved not ourselves disorderly among you" (2 Thes 3:6, 7).

Disorderly means lazy, but this is the verse where Danielle's church teaches her not to keep company with sinners. They teach that people who are sinning are walking disorderly. She is told to withdraw from them.

Paul is actually telling us to withdraw from lazy busybodies, gossipers, and tale-bearers. They go house to house or call on the phone. They pass all the goose juice and eat and drink for free. Often, you'll find them down on their luck and using others for money, food, and shelter. Paul says that he set a good example. He never went around gossiping or getting free food and drinks while preaching the gospel.

"Neither did we eat any man's bread for nought; but wrought with labour and travail night and day, that we might not be chargeable to any of you: Not because we have not power, but to make ourselves an ensample unto you to follow us" (2 Thes 3:8, 9).

Paul wasn't lazy. He was a tentmaker and worked hard to earn his own way. He was not disorderly, meaning he wasn't a lazy busybody. Paul says that God's servants deserve a fair salary from the congregation. However, so he wouldn't burden the people, he earned his own money by making and selling his tents.

"For even when we were with you, this we commanded you, that if any would not work, neither should he eat. For we hear that there are some which walk among you disorderly, working not at all, but are busybodies" (2 Thes 3:10, 11).

Disorderly means being a lazy busybody. Gossipers, or tale-bearers, who spread false tales. People who won't work shouldn't eat. Nobody likes lazy fuddy-duddies. Don't let others use us. If they don't work, they don't get our freebies. And I don't want their goose juice either!

"Now them that are such we command and exhort by our Lord Jesus Christ, that with quietness they work, and eat their own bread. But ye, brethren, be not weary in well doing" (2 Thes 3:12, 13).

Paul was saying, "Stop gossiping, get to work, and earn your own way." We aren't supposed to help lazy busybodies. However, we should continue to help others who sometimes face hardships.

"And if any man obey not our word by this epistle, note that man, and have no company with him, that he may be ashamed" (2 Thes 3:14).

If anyone does not obey our word — not to be a lazy busybody — then do not associate with them. We are to distance ourselves from gossiping, backbiting, and contentious busybodies. They stir the pot and cause division.

Danielle's church focuses on verses six and fourteen. Meanwhile, they skip the entire busybody part of the story. They don't teach that Paul is addressing the gossipers here. They claim Paul is telling them to withdraw from all sinners, which doesn't even make sense. Jesus ate with sinners and came to save them from perishing. Preaching the kingdom of heaven literally involves going among sinners to teach them about Jesus and His love for us.

Danielle rebukes people for their sins. If the sinner doesn't obey, she shakes the dust off her feet and abandons them. Sheesh! As if she's not a sinner too? Paul was actually saying not to keep company with gossipers. So, since Danielle gossips, Paul is telling me to admonish her. If she doesn't obey his words and stop, then I shouldn't hang out with her.

It's unwise to befriend someone who gossips. Those who sit and talk with you about others will also talk with others about you.

"Yet count him not as an enemy, but admonish him as a brother" (2 Thes 3:15).

This verse doesn't give us permission to admonish sinners. Paul is actually telling us to admonish the gossipers and tale-bearers. He said to do so kindly, with brotherly love. Tell them we are no longer interested in their goose juice.

Don't invite the geese-ipers into your home. Refrain from giving them coffee and cookies when they stop by to chat. Don't answer the phone when they call. Tell them, "The devil finds work for idle hands." Say, "The harder you work, the luckier you will get." Tell them that gossiping and spreading rumors are harmful half-truths and fall under the "Thou shalt not bear false witness" commandment. Let them know that you no longer wish to participate.

If we cherry-pick Bible verses without reading the entire story, we'll misinterpret the message. We will admonish the wrong people. If a geese-iper reads the story correctly, they would have to admonish themselves.

"Whosoever therefore shall break one of these least commandments, and shall teach men so, he shall be called the least in the kingdom of heaven: but whosoever shall do and teach them, the same shall be called great in the kingdom of heaven" (Mt 5:19).

People who teach their children to gossip will be the least in the kingdom of heaven — if they make it there. To be the greatest, we must obey our Father's house rules. Father considers them the least if they teach others that they can break some commandments. This means that all commandments are equal, and we can't teach others that it's okay to break any of them.

Gossiping often reveals low self-esteem and feelings of guilt. These individuals highlight the sins of others. This behavior is an attempt to boost their sense of superiority over the person they gossip about. The more they tarnish others' reputations, the better they feel about their chances of going to heaven.

Geese-ipers have a strong addiction to the juice. They love hearing bad things about others because it gives them an adrenaline rush and a mental high of feeling better than others. That high is short-lived because their self-worth is so low. They continuously hunt for more juice to give themselves another boost. It's always a mad dash to get another adrenaline rush — to feel that high again.

They repeat every rumor and add their own speculations as they pass it to the next set of eager ears. They can't wait for you to leave so they can make that phone call to pass it along. Gossipers would rather die than miss a call. That would mean missing out on the next bit of juicy gossip.

Their preacher never delivers sermons about gossip. He wants to stay informed. The gossip gives him plenty of guilt-trip ideas for his sermons. It's best to stop minding other people's affairs, stop listening to geese-ipers, and stop passing along false witness. Otherwise, Father will take out His handy little juicer, and He will juice your goose!

~ Goose Juice ~

Only fools meddle in other people's business. Only fools grab and pull a dog's ears. Both actions will get you bitten. If you meddle in my affairs and tell me what I should or shouldn't do in my personal life — if you pull my ears — there's a good chance I'll bite you.

"He that passeth by, and meddleth with strife belonging not to him, is like one that taketh a dog by the ears" (Prov 26:17).

If you poke a stick at a wounded animal, it will bite you. Poking sticks into people's wounds isn't the correct way to help them heal.

"Where no wood is, there the fire goeth out: so where there is no talebearer, the strife ceaseth" (Prov 26:20).

Gossiping tale-bearers and busybodies cause strife. If there were no gossipers, there would be no strife. It's simple: stop gossiping, and the conflict will end.

As coals are to burning coals, and wood to fire; so is a contentious man to kindle strife" (Prov 26:21).

Geese-ipers are contentious people. They love to keep the fire burning. They enjoy stirring the pot and keeping everyone fired up.

"The words of a talebearer are as wounds, and they go down into the innermost parts of the belly" (Prov 26:22).

Tale-bearers inflict deep wounds with their words. They drag a person's name through the mud. Their stories are partly lies. It traumatizes the hearts of their victims and damages their reputation and livelihood.

"Burning lips and a wicked heart are like a potsherd covered with silver dross" (Prov 26:23).

Father has negative feelings about people who gossip. A potsherd is a toilet. You can make a toilet look fancy by covering it with silver dross. People wear fancy clothing and hats to church. Gossipers have wicked hearts with burning lips. In Poppa's eyes, they are still just a filthy toilet. Father has some funny analogies.

"Ye blind guides, which strain at a gnat, and swallow a camel" (Mt 23:24).

The scribes and Pharisees constantly nitpicked other people's minor sins and were self-righteous about their own major sins.

> Woe onto you, scribes and Pharisees, hypocrites! For ye make clean the outside of the cup and of the platter, but within they are full of extortion and excess. Thou blind Pharisee, cleanse first that which is within the cup and platter, that the outside of them

> may be clean also. Woe unto you, scribes and Pharisees, hypocrites! for ye are like unto whited sepulchers, which indeed appear beautiful outward, but are within full of dead men's bones, and of all uncleanness. Even so ye also outwardly appear righteous unto men, but within ye are full of hypocrisy and iniquity. (Mt 23:25-28)

It's like putting lipstick on a pig — on the outside, they look as beautiful as a decorated, fancy gravestone. Still, inside the beautiful coffin, they are spiritually dead. Deep down, they are mean, lofty, self-righteous, judgmental, critical, filthy toilets covered with a shiny silver coating. They can go hog wild washing and decorating the exterior of their bodies. Still, Father sees their filthy, self-righteous hearts. He regards them as nothing more than a muddy pig in a blanket.

Unless we clean the inside of our hearts, we are hypocrites — filthy, disgusting, spiritually dead, decorated toilets.

"For I say unto you, That except your righteousness shall exceed the righteousness of the scribes and Pharisees, ye shall in no case enter into the kingdom of heaven" (Mt 5:20).

Pigs will fly before these self-righteous people enter heaven. They believed that nitpicking others was the way to get into heaven. They were as happy as pigs in mud as they sat in Moses' seat, judging and condemning everyone.

"Thou shalt not bear false witness against thy neighbour" (Ex 20:16).

"The lip of truth shall be established for ever: but a lying tongue is but for a moment. Lying lips are abomination to the Lord: but they that deal truly are his delight" (Prov 12:19, 22).

"If any man among you seem to be religious, and bridleth not his tongue, but deceiveth his own heart, this man's religion is vain" (Jas 1:26).

A gossiper's religion is vain — pretend — and not real. They have not bridled their tongues. They are pretending to be Christians. If Jesus were in their hearts, they wouldn't be so frivolous about hurting His kids.

"Out of the same mouth proceedeth blessing and cursing. My brethren, these things ought not so to be" (Jas 3:10).

These goose-ipers don't check if the information they eagerly listen to is accurate. In a gossip community, all it takes is one person to have the goose juice, and the phones will ring all day long as each goose-iper spews the new goose juice to everyone else.

"The aged women likewise, that they be in behaviour as becometh holiness, not false accusers, not given to much wine, teachers of good things" (Tit 2:3).

"But let none of you suffer as a murderer, or as a thief, or as an evildoer, or as a busybody in other men's matters" (1 Pet 4:15).

Interestingly, the meddling busybody gossiper is mentioned in the same verse as the murderer, the thief, and the evildoer.

"Beware of false prophets, which come to you in sheep's clothing, but inwardly they are ravening wolves. Ye shall know them by their fruits. Do men gather grapes of thorns, or figs of thistles?" (Mt 7:15, 16).

> Wherefore by their fruits ye shall know them. Not every one that saith unto me, Lord, Lord, shall enter into the kingdom of heaven; but he that doeth the will of my Father which is in heaven. Many will say to me in that day, Lord, Lord, have we not prophesied in thy name? and in thy name have cast out devils? and in thy name done many wonderful works? And then will I profess unto them, I never knew you: depart from me, ye that work iniquity. (Mt 7:20-23)

These fake Christians didn't cast out devils, nor did they perform many wonderful works. They were pretend Christians and were only going through the motions of church.

Jesus says that wise people who follow His teachings have built their house on a rock. Their foundation is solid, and they will stand. Foolish people, who don't do His works of love, have their homes built on sand. Their foundation is weak, and they will fall.

We'll know if a person has Jesus in their life by how they treat others. Jesus doesn't gossip or speak malicious words. He doesn't look haughtily down His nose at sinners. Jesus doesn't act too righteous to be near sinners. Holier-than-thou people won't enter heaven. Father will juice their goose!

~ Golden Goose ~

Many religions believe they possess the golden goose that grants them the exclusive path to heaven. As Satan intended, this causes dissension, arguments, and religious hierarchy. Many consider themselves more special than others outside their specific denomination.

We should abandon all religious labels created by men or their theology. For example, Calvinist refers to people who follow John Calvin's teachings. Danielle is following an offshoot of Calvinism. Those who follow Christ and His teachings call themselves Christians. We should only identify as a Christ-ian, meaning Christ-man, Christ-woman, or Christ-child.

Many today claim they are Christians, but they aren't obeying the first commandment, which states to love our Father with our whole heart, soul, strength, and mind. They also do not follow the second commandment, which is to love our neighbors as we love ourselves.

Love, in a nutshell, is the entire Ten Commandments. Jesus said that when we love Him, then we will obey His commandments of love. The opposite is also true: those who don't love Him will not follow His love commandments. The only way to gain eternal life is to follow Poppa's rules of love.

To teach the Bible effectively, we first need to read, study, and thoroughly understand it.

"Study to shew thyself approved unto God, a workman that needeth not to be ashamed, rightly dividing the word of truth" (2 Tim 2:15).

Some churches teach a soft, lazy, and lukewarm 'just believe' doctrine. Others, like John Calvin, teach a doctrine filled with hellfire, damnation, guilt, shame, and fear. They all claim to have the golden goose.

The lukewarm churches claim that you're saved simply by believing in Jesus. Believing in what exactly? Satan also believes Jesus is real. He won't attain salvation. They also tell their congregation that we're saved by faith alone, not by works. However, I've read various stories and verses in the Bible that disagree.

The story of the ten virgins includes five foolish Christians. When the Bridegroom — Jesus — returned, He did not allow them to enter the marriage chamber. They believed in Jesus, but they didn't have enough oil in their lamps. They talk the talk, but they don't walk the walk. Their lamps didn't have sufficient truth, repentance, and love. They didn't follow Father's path:

"Afterward came also the other virgins, saying, Lord, Lord, open to us. But he answered and said, Verily I say unto you, I know you not" (Mt 25:11, 12).

These five foolish pretend-Christian virgins only went through the motions of church. They had one foot in church and the other in the world. They attended church sometimes, but they spent the rest of their time gossiping, watching sinful content on TV, listening to vulgar, negative, and perverted music, partying, cursing, and acting like brute beasts. These foolish virgins didn't circumcise their hearts and didn't strive to live a pure lifestyle. They believed that playing church would get them into heaven.

They foolishly thought it was okay to serve both masters. They never gave themselves to our Master — Jesus — who died, gave His life, and allowed Himself to be tortured and murdered. Giving 5% of their time to Father and 95% to Satan, they followed the filth that the enemy offered them.

They didn't become grieved for their worship of celebrities, musicians, clothing, hairstyles, and sports players. They didn't care that they were putting all these things first and placing Poppa last. Our Father, who created them, loves them, and provides shelter, food, and water, gets last place.

To become wise virgins, we must purify our hearts and love our Poppa. We must do the things He said to do. Being a Christian isn't a part-time, once-a-week event of going to church on Sunday. It's a daily effort to please Father and perform as many good, loving works as possible.

Only the people who love, thank, trust, serve, obey, and prioritize Him in their lives will spend eternity with Him. If people could see the gifts in store for us who love and serve Him — they would give up everything to seek Him.

The Bible is explicit that everyone will be "judged out of those things which were written in the books, according to their works ... and they were judged every man according to their works" (Rev 20:12, 13).

We should ensure we have excellent works written behind our names. On Judgment Day, we will receive a massive payout for all our acts of love. Payday also includes clothing, for "the fine linen is the righteousness of saints" (Rev 19:8).

The more righteous acts — the more acts of love we perform — the finer linen garments we will receive as our reward when we enter the Pearly Gates of heaven.

I'm sure the geese-ipers won't have very many fine linen garments in heaven — if they make it there. We will see the distinction between the least and the greatest by the number of garments being worn. Some people might be as naked as a baby jaybird. That will be quite an interesting sight to see. It's necessary to follow Father's house rules — our clothing depends on it!

"Think not that I am come to destroy the law, or the prophets: I am not come to destroy, but to fulfil. For verily I say unto you, Till heaven and earth pass, one jot or one tittle shall in no wise pass from the law, till all be fulfilled" (Mt 5:17, 18).

Jesus did not destroy, alter, or remove the law. He didn't change the law in the slightest — not one word or punctuation mark. Love will be required of us forever. We'd best get crackin'! Practice makes perfect!

Many have never learned to follow the subject and object when reading the Bible. They read a few verses and create their own interpretations as they go. As we see in the following verses, when we read carefully, Father's Word takes on a whole new meaning:

"We then, as workers together with him … But in all things approving ourselves as the ministers of God … Be ye not unequally yoked together with unbelievers: for what fellowship hath righteousness with unrighteousness? and what communion hath light with darkness?" (2 Cor 6:1, 4, 14).

The subject is workers — servants alongside Jesus, or those who teach and serve God's Word. We must not yoke up with nonbelievers to teach God's Word. Those in darkness do not have God's light inside them. They are a goose on the loose and are on a wild goose chase, following every whim of the world. Wild geese worship people, pagan holidays, and material things.

It would be like trying to catch a muddy pig if we use them as helpers. Until they grasp how to read correctly, they stay in darkness and are of no help to you while you're teaching.

Danielle believes that anyone outside her church is an unbeliever. Therefore, she interprets this verse to mean that she should not associate with outsiders. She missed the subject of the story. She thinks it means she is not to fellowship with anyone who doesn't believe what her church teaches — even family.

"And what concord hath Christ with Belial? or what part hath he that believeth with an infidel? And what agreement hath the temple of God with idols? for ye are the temple of the living God; as God hath said, I will dwell in them, and walk in them; and I will be their God, and they shall be my people. Wherefore come out from among them, and be ye separate, saith the Lord, and touch not the unclean thing; and I will receive you" (2 Cor 6:15, 16, 17).

"Touch not the unclean thing" means that when we go out to teach God's Word, we can't attach ourselves to idol worshippers. They live in darkness and follow a belief system that conflicts with the Bible. We are not to yoke ourselves with unbelievers when ministering, teaching, or preaching God's Word.

When we yoke oxen together, they each pull half the load of the plow. The same concept applies when teaching God's Word: both workers must work together in cooperation. If two people yoked together hold opposing beliefs, they won't be in harmony. Instead, they will only confuse and pull the new person in the opposite direction.

For example, an opportunity might arise to teach someone about Passover and how Jesus instructed us to celebrate it until He returns. When you go out to teach, don't team up with someone who, instead of celebrating Passover, observes the pagan holiday of Ishtar. They wouldn't be a helpful teammate, as they are not in harmony with your teaching. They wouldn't assist you in explaining Passover. Instead, they'd be more of an anchor to you. They would prevent you from explaining that the word 'Easter' appears only once in the Bible, and that it is a mistranslation.

In the KJV's Strong's Exhaustive Concordance of the Bible, the Greek word for Easter is Pascha (G3957). Pascha means Passover. The Wycliffe Bible is an earlier translation and does not use the word Easter at all; instead, it uses the word Pask, which also translates as Passover. The Latin Vulgate Bible is an even older version and uses the word Pasch, which means Passover.

Easter originates from the word Ishtar. Ishtar is the pagan goddess of fertility. People celebrated spring festivals in her honor. These festivals included orgies at the temple of Ishtar. The bunny and eggs also carry significance. We are all aware of how rapidly rabbits reproduce. We've heard what it means to hop like a bunny. The Easter eggs symbolize fertility eggs inside a woman's womb.

The unbeliever that Father warned us not to yoke ourselves with would only cause arguments and disagreements when you teach about the Passover. Wolves in sheep's clothing have brainwashed the unbelievers. They now believe God told them to roll Easter eggs and wear bunny costumes on His most holy High Sabbath Day.

Passover was the day Jesus died on the cross. He hung there and bled to death. Satan has hijacked Passover and mixed it with the pagan festival of worshiping Ishtar. Not only are people hopping like bunnies and rolling their colorful fertility eggs, but they also celebrate it on a completely different day than what our Father commanded us to observe Passover.

Passover is the day Jesus had those large nails driven through His hands and feet — the same day they tortured Him and hanged Him on that old rugged cross. Many churches also go out early on the morning of Ishtar for a sunrise worship service. That leads down a whole different rabbit hole, as this practice originates from another pagan ritual of sun worship.

We are to celebrate Passover to remember how Jesus became the Sacrificial Lamb and paid our death penalty for us. To teach this, we can't yoke together with an unbeliever who celebrates Ishtar. We must not participate in all their fluff and stuff that accompanies their pagan goddess worship.

Instead of dedicating a day to gratitude and remembering Jesus, they teach children it's just a fun day filled with bunnies, eggs, and candy. We couldn't explain Passover to a newcomer without the unbeliever scoffing and arguing during the lesson. Don't yoke yourself with an unbeliever to teach God's Word. Their oppositional anchor will only weigh us down. They would pull us and the new person in opposite directions, making our teaching ineffective.

What connection, harmony, or alliance does Jesus have with Ishtar, the goddess of fertility? Belial means wicked or worthless. Christians celebrate Passover. Celebrating Ishtar has nothing to do with Jesus. When teaching God's Word, don't attach yourself to Ishtar worshipers. They'll be worthless to you. "Touch not the unclean thing" means don't participate with them in their unclean practices. The temple of God — His servants — has no agreement with the idol Ishtar. She doesn't lay golden eggs. Jesus is the Golden Goose who owns all the golden eggs.

These passages don't mean we should separate ourselves from all sinners or abandon our blood relatives. It didn't say to disassociate with people who are not members of our specific church or don't share our beliefs. Christians are Jesus' servants. Their job is to lead sinners to Jesus. We can't share Father's love with people if we abandon them in a better-than-thou, haughty manner.

Danielle looks down on everyone who believes differently from her. She thinks her church people are the only ones who will go to heaven. Meanwhile, she closes her eyes, repeats empty repetitions, engages in lengthy prayers, argues about dogma, worships Ishtar, and follows made-up church traditions.

Danielle celebrates Ishtar. She doesn't know that she is the unclean thing that the servants of Jesus are told "not to touch" or "attach themselves to" when they preach God's Word.

~ Golden Eggs ~

Father has a nice list and a naughty list. Let's see what else gets us put on His naughty list:

> I have spread out my hands all the day unto a rebellious people, which walketh in a way that was not good, after their own thoughts; … A people that provoketh me to anger continually to my face; … which eat swine's flesh, and broth of abominable things is in their vessels; Which say, Stand by thyself, come not near to me; for I am holier than thou. These are a smoke in my nose, a fire that burneth all the day. Behold, it is written before me: I will not keep silence, but will recompense, even recompense into their bosom. (Is 65:2-6)

Those who eat swine's flesh and exude a holier-than-thou attitude are a smoke in Father's nose. These two things cause Him severe irritation. Imagine smoke filling your nose every day — that's how offensive these are to Him.

I'm sure committing sacrilege by desecrating Passover and instead celebrating Ishtar, a pagan fertility goddess holiday, also irritates our Father's nose. Then, to make things worse, many people, after their Ishtar church service, go home to prepare a feast with a great big ol' swine's flesh ham.

Father told us that exuding a Holy Joe attitude, eating swine's flesh, worshipping Ishtar, judging others, being condescending, self-righteous, and hateful are a constant, irritating smoke in His nose. Just like when a cow gets chaff in its nose, Father will soon snort that irritating smoke out with force. His wrath will splatter onto all who engage in such things. When Father sneezes to clear that filthy irritation out of His nose, we'd better watch out. The shizzy is going to hit the fizzy, and the whole show is gonna blow.

Divorce isn't the worst sin, nor is it equal to the unforgivable one. I've read nowhere in the Bible where God said divorce is a constant irritation in His nostrils. Many people believe they have the golden goose that lays golden eggs, yet they don't follow our Father's health laws. What a mockery! What an insult to Poppa! They believe Father told Peter it's now okay to eat unclean swine's flesh, but with basic reading skills, we can see this isn't true:

> Peter went up upon the housetop to pray about the sixth hour: And he became very hungry, and would have eaten: but while they made ready, he fell into a trance, And saw heaven opened, and a certain vessel descending upon him, as it had been a great sheet knit at the four corners, and let down to the earth: Wherein were all manner of four footed beasts of the earth, and wild beasts, and creeping things, and fowls of the air. And there came a voice to him, Rise, Peter; kill, and eat. But Peter said, Not so, Lord; for I have never eaten any thing that is common or unclean. And the voice spake unto him again the second time, What God hath cleansed, that call not thou common. This was done thrice: and the vessel

> was received up again into heaven. Now while Peter doubted in himself what this vision which he had seen should mean. (Acts 10:9-17)

Peter was contemplating what the vision might mean. All visions and dreams from God contain hidden messages. Every parable teaches a lesson. Danielle thinks Peter's vision implies that God declared all unclean animals to be clean. She says we can now eat unclean animals. However, she didn't read the rest of the chapter to find out the actual message. She never discovered the golden egg, which reveals the real meaning of Peter's vision.

"And he said unto them, Ye know how that it is an unlawful thing for a man that is a Jew to keep company, or come unto one of another nation; but God hath shewed me that I should not call any man common or unclean" (Acts 10:28).

Peter did not eat any of the unclean animals in his vision. God lifted them all back into heaven. Peter was specific. He said God showed him in the vision that he was not to call any person common or unclean.

The reason non-Israelite nations were called unclean or uncommon wasn't because they were dirty or less deserving of God's love. It was because Jesus needed to be born through a pure, unmixed bloodline. The Israelites were not to intermarry with other nations so that Jesus could be born from the tribe of Judah and of Levi. Jesus fulfilled the prophecy that He would be a High Priest forever after the order of Melchizedek.

Now that Jesus had been born, the mission was complete. His disciples were to go to all nations to preach to them about Jesus. There was no longer a threat of Jesus' bloodline being destroyed through intermixing. Father sent His golden egg. Jesus was born and died on the cross. In fulfilling this prophecy, Jesus destroyed death, which is to say, the Devil.

Our Father didn't waste His time telling us which animals and fish are clean and unclean. Swine wallow in and eat each other's manure. They eat every rotten and disgusting thing they find. God created the unclean scavengers to clean up the earth, roadkill, and waters. They eat anything, no matter how decayed. Pigs lack multiple stomachs or gizzards to filter out the bacteria, worms, and parasites they consume. Father even warned us not to touch the dead carcasses of these filthy scavengers. They don't have sweat glands to eliminate the toxins they ingest. Everything they eat goes straight into their meat. Mmmm. Nummy.

Many false prophets tell their parishioners that God has cleansed all the filthy, manure-eating swine. Many serve this scavenger animal as their main delicacy at their Ishtar feasts. Sleep on, sweet Jezebel. The deception is strong. Many people undergo intense brainwashing. They don't realize that their false prophet preacher is the dressed-up wolves that Jesus warned us about.

Father puts a spirit of slumber upon everyone who does not have a love for the truth. They will not study. Instead, they love their religious superiority, gossip, judging, eating swine, long repetitious prayers, rituals, Ishtar feasts, and made-up church traditions. If they loved our Father, they would read His letter and obey Him.

Passover began when the thirteen tribes of Israel left slavery in Egypt. God instructed them to put blood on their doorposts as an act of obedience. That was so that the Angel of Death would pass over their homes and spare their firstborn children. God commanded them to observe Passover every year, starting on the fourteenth day after the spring equinox in the evening. They brought offerings to the priest for the forgiveness of their sins. They celebrated Passover to remember the promised Messiah, who would come and sacrifice Himself as the Lamb to pay for their sins. On Judgment Day, the Death Angel will pass over those with Jesus' blood on the doorpost of their heart.

"And this day shall be unto you for a memorial; and ye shall keep it a feast to the Lord throughout your generations; ye shall keep it a feast by an ordinance for ever" (Exodus 12:14).

Father commanded us to keep the Feast of Passover forever! The word 'forever' is specific. There shouldn't be any confusion about its meaning. He didn't say to celebrate the swine-infested, pagan orgy festival honoring Ishtar, the goddess of fertility, forever. The false prophets don't tell their followers the true meaning of the word 'forever.'

I'm sure Danielle believes she'll be in heaven, and I won't be there with her. I'm not a member of her "God's only truth" church. Perchance Danielle thinks I'll be there too; she doesn't see us together. She sees herself in a different part of heaven than where I would be.

She will get to live in the special area reserved for the exceptionally righteous people. There, they can gossip and eat swine's flesh as they hold pagan rituals in the woods to honor the goddess Ishtar. These holy individuals will hop around like bunnies, and their golden goose will continually lay its golden eggs of fertility.

God's true church isn't a building. Being a Christian is not specific to membership in a building. Christianity isn't a religion; it's a reality. The true church of Jesus is a worldwide, many-member body of people who love Father and become His servants.

Every day, we sigh and long for Jesus to return so we can be close to Him. Every day, we pray for that beautiful day when wickedness and perversion are gone.

We tell our Poppa: "You are the Potter, and I am the clay. Use me for whatever you need today. You lead, I will follow. Use me for what you need tomorrow. I am yours, and you are mine. Whatever you have for me to do is fine. You are my Father, I am your child. Always keep us reconciled. You are my Master, and I am your maid. Under your shade, I am not afraid."

We enjoy serving Him and want to help in any way we can. Being peaceful, we go with His flow; we let Him lead us as Father always knows best.

Father wants all of His children to turn their hearts toward Him, to love and worship Him. He loves them all. He wants us to turn away from the harmful, evil, vulgar, and perverted things of this world. The punishment for sin is death. Jesus permitted evil people to put Him to death. He paid the penalty of death for us.

Father sent us the Bible. When we read and study His letter, it helps us build a strong relationship with Him. As we read, we pray with a sincere desire for wisdom, knowledge, and understanding. Our Father's Spirit prompts thoughts, raises questions, and provides answers. After reading His beautiful love letter, we understand how much He loves us and how that love is the key to heaven.

The intense love that Poppa has for us is impossible to grasp. Anyone can choose to have a Poppa-child relationship with Him. Just start talking to Him. He's waiting for us to come to Him. Be honest about all our shortcomings and mistakes. He already knows them all.

Father won't force us to love Him. He won't make us choose the good. We get to decide where our happily or not-so-happily-ever-afters will be. We are in the flesh spotlight. Everything we do, think, and speak is being kept track of by our Heavenly Father. Let's make Him proud of us.

~ Master Goose ~

Poppa came to Earth and entered a flesh body. His name is Jesus, Immanuel, or God with us:

"In the beginning was the Word, and the Word was with God, and the Word was God. And the Word was made flesh, and dwelt among us" (Jn 1:1, 14).

"I and my Father are one" (Jn 10:30).

"He that hath seen me hath seen the Father; and how sayest thou then, Show us the Father?" (Jn 14:9).

Jesus is Father. Jesus is our Creator. Father, the Word, became flesh and dwelt among us. Our Father entered a fleshly body. Jesus is the Living Word:

"Therefore the Lord himself shall give you a sign; Behold, a virgin shall conceive, and bear a son, and shall call his name Immanuel" (Is 7:14).

"Behold, a virgin shall be with child, and shall bring forth a son, and they shall call his name Emmanuel, which being interpreted is, God with us" (Mt 1:23).

Jesus, still teaching us while He was dying, used His last breath to tell us to read Psalm 22. He pointed us to the detailed prophecy of His crucifixion nearly 1000 years earlier:

"And about the ninth hour Jesus cried with a loud voice, saying, Eli, Eli, lama sabachthani? That is to say, My God, my God, why hast thou forsaken me?" (Mt 27:46).

God did not forsake Jesus. God is Jesus. He was telling us His prophecy is now fulfilled. He was saying to read:

> My God, my God, why hast thou forsaken me? They gaped upon me with their mouths, as a ravening and a roaring lion. I am poured out like water, and all my bones are out of joint: my heart is like wax; it is melted in the midst of my bowels. My strength is dried up like a potsherd; and my tongue cleaveth to my jaws; and thou hast brought me into the dust of death. For dogs have compassed me: the assembly of the wicked have enclosed me: they pierced my hands and my feet. I may tell all my bones: they look and stare upon me. They part my garments among them, and cast lots upon my vesture. (Ps 22:1, 13-18)

This prophecy of Jesus being nailed to the cross came true exactly as predicted. It was very detailed, right down to the Roman soldiers casting lots for His garments. That proves to us that Father is in complete control. He is the Master Goose. He will carry out His entire Master Plan exactly as He has designed and prophesied.

Father forced the Roman soldiers to cast lots. It was to show us that He is real and that what He prophesied will always come to pass. Remember when Father hardened Pharaoh's heart in Egypt? Father can force us to do anything. We are tiny ants compared to Him. Little ants that Satan is trying to squash.

Isaiah gives us more prophecy about how Jesus was to come as the sacrifice to pay for our transgressions:

> He was oppressed, and he was afflicted, yet he opened not his mouth: he is brought as a lamb to the slaughter, and as a sheep before her shearers is dumb, so he openeth not his mouth. He was taken from prison and from judgment: and who shall declare his generation? for he was cut off out of the land of the living: for the transgression of my people was he stricken. And he made his grave with the wicked, and with the rich in his death; because he had done no violence, neither was any deceit in his mouth. (Is 53:7-9)

Jesus didn't open His mouth. He didn't defend Himself. He knew He came to die for all who would love Him. Jesus died with wicked malefactors beside Him. They buried Him with the wealthy. Joseph of Arimathea was Jesus' uncle. He was a wealthy man. Joseph buried Jesus in his fancy tomb.

We are Poppa's little plants. Satan is poisoning us with his evil. He despises Father and seeks to hurt Him by poisoning and infesting His little plants. Satan poisons them with gossip, evil, vulgar, perverted television shows, indecent movies, crass music, rebellious behaviors, pagan holiday worship, lying, cheating, stealing, killing, murdering, drugs, alcohol, worshiping celebrities, judging, criticizing, division, derision, and religious hierarchy. All who do not have Jesus to deflect the fiery darts are vulnerable to Satan's perverse suggestions, infestations, and temptations.

Satan is so perverted and deceptive that he makes the little infested plants believe their infestation is fun and cool. The only cure for the infestation is to put our roots into Jesus. He is the Master Vine. He is pure and holy. Only Jesus can purge the infestation from us as He intertwines, purifies, and cleanses us.

Only healthy, non-infested plants may enter heaven. Our magnificent Father doesn't want or need poisoned or infested plants. He will throw all infested plants onto the burn pile. Every plant can uproot itself and walk right up to the Master Vine. They can ask Father to plant their roots in Him. If they refuse to uproot themselves, the day will come when Father uproots them. He will cast them into the fire, so they can't harm His other plants anymore.

Imagine the field as Earth. Satan is on one side, spreading his filthy infestations over everyone. Then picture Jesus on the other side. He has His arms wide open, offering peace and protection to anyone who desires it. Part of Satan's infestation includes his deception to make people believe that Jesus' side is boring.

Father owns the field and has many servants — under a bubble of His protection — working out there in His field. Father gave us orders to inform all the infested plants that Jesus is offering them safety and protection from the evil enemy's infestations. His servants are trying to show all the little plants how to uproot themselves from the muddy, murky, filthy, infested swamp. They can just walk over to

Jesus and root themselves in Him. He will help them get cleaned up.

"But as it is written, Eye hath not seen, nor ear heard, neither have entered into the heart of man, the things which God hath prepared for them that love him" (1 Cor 2:9).

Incentives influence behavior. Perhaps some plants haven't heard about the wonderful things waiting for us in heaven. To receive those blessings and rewards, we must uproot ourselves from Satan's swamp and choose to love our Poppa. The eye has not seen, nor ear heard. It hasn't even entered our minds. We can't imagine all the marvelous things our Father has prepared for us.

Let's imagine the incredible things Father has planned for us. What He secretly has in store is a trillion times more amazing. The Bible says we will have a new heaven and a new earth. Father will restore everything to its original, perfect state. Everything will be lush and green, filled with beautiful flowers, plants, and trees. Perfect weather will last all year, with no storms. Darkness and night will disappear. The sun will provide perfect radiant warmth year-round, so there will be no more extreme weather. Our toes won't freeze in winter. Every day, a perfect amount of water will fall from heaven to nourish all of our Father's beautiful creations. Imagine never having to deal with weeds again!

We'll have perfect soil for gardening, allowing us to grow a limitless variety of vegetables and fruit trees. Since we'll all be in spiritual bodies, we'll also be eating manna. In heaven, there's likely an array of incredible foods we've never seen or even imagined could exist. Our spiritual bodies will never age, get sick, or die. Everyone will have perfect peace, joy, love, and happiness.

Heaven will not have any vulgarity, perversion, or perverted talk — no deception, corruption, thieves, liars, gossipers, talebearers, or false witnesses. Wars, hate, racism, bigotry, drugs, alcoholics, or murderers won't exist. Forget about boredom and lazy people. Best of all, no taxes ever again!

Every good thing we enjoy now, we will also enjoy in heaven. Everything good and beautiful will remain when Jesus returns to Earth. He will only destroy and remove evil things and evil people. We will enjoy endless gardening, golfing, and every beautiful instrument, including pianos and organs. We'll create stunning artistic masterpieces, whether through music, painting, constructing streets of gold, or building majestic structures and bridges.

We might communicate by reading each other's minds through extrasensory perception, speaking via a quantum energy field of sorts. Our amazing, super-speedy flying vehicles will run on free and clean energy. We'll enjoy unlimited travel anywhere on Earth and in space. If we dream big, many inter-dimensional adventures could be in our future.

Saving the best for last, we'll enjoy a wonderful, beautiful, amazing, personal, unlimited Father-child relationship with Poppa! Our amazing Poppa will spoil us rotten and give us all His most wonderful gifts — all because we love Him, respect Him, and follow His easy House Rules.

These are the things I imagine our Poppa has prepared for us. It will be a trillion times more amazing and magical. He said we can't even imagine all the wonderful things He has in store for us. I'm excited. To me, it's like waiting for the biggest and best Christmas morning to arrive — and it can't come soon enough!

"Blessed and holy is he that hath part in the first resurrection: on such the second death hath no power, but they shall be priests of God and of Christ, and shall reign with him a thousand years" (Rev 20:6).

If we are serious about this and overcome Satan and his infestation now, before Jesus returns, we'll be stamped as overcomers. The flesh death is the first death. The second death is the death of our soul. Overcomers will never again have to worry about the death of their souls.

The first resurrection occurs when Jesus arrives on Earth. Those who overcome are those who love Him. They have uprooted themselves from Satan's filth-infested world and have rooted themselves in Jesus. The overcomers live their lives for Him. They will not worship or fall for Satan's deception as the antichrist. The overcomers will refuse to become a part of Satan's false one-world political, financial, and religious peace system. The overcomers will pass the test. They will live and reign on Earth with Jesus for 1000 years. They will have earned eternal life in that beautiful place called Heaven.

"To him that overcometh, will I grant to sit with me in my throne, even as I also overcame, and am sat down with my father in his throne" (Rev 3:21).

Those who overcome "lived and reigned with Christ a thousand years" (Rev 20:4).

Only the overcomers will live with Jesus during the one thousand years. To overcome means loving our Papa with all our heart, soul, strength, and mind. It also involves loving everything Father loves and hating all things that Father hates.

These thousand years are the millennium. It is the Lord's Day. It remains a time of teaching, preaching, and salvation. Our Father is a patient and loving God. He gives the children who have not overcome Satan an extra thousand years to get their act together. During this period, Father locks Satan away in the pit. He can no longer influence, deceive, or corrupt the little plants.

Those who don't overcome Satan will have to be tested again at the end of the thousand years. Father will release Satan out of the pit for a short time. Anyone who overcomes Satan at that time will receive eternal life. These thousand years serve as a testing period without Satan's influence. We must be tested and proven to show our Father who we are.

During the millennium, the overcomers can visit their families who didn't overcome. That is to teach them discipline and show them how to love. We'll encourage them to choose behaviors that are not harmful to our Father, themselves, or others. Only loving people can enter heaven.

After the millennium, Father will briefly release Satan from the pit. I felt flabbergasted to learn that the followers of Satan will still be as numerous as the sand of the sea!

Then, finally, Judgment Day. Each child will stand before Father. Judgment isn't a group trial. Every person must answer individually for their actions, thoughts, and words.

Everyone will face the music. Father will blot out all who refuse to love Him — those who love Satan and his evil, demonic, harmful behavior. Father will turn them to ashes from within.

We will never have to tolerate bad behavior again. The wicked people love their behavior. Otherwise, they would have given it up by the time Judgment Day arrives. What a day of rejoicing it will be. Peace, joy, love, and happiness forever and ever.

Satan's wolves have lied, claiming that you can't choose to love Poppa. They also stated that pigs are clean animals suitable for consumption. If that's your cup of tea, if that's what you believe Father told us to do, then eat to your heart's content. If you think He said to celebrate the pagan goddess Ishtar holiday instead of Passover, if you wish to gossip, backbite, pillage, steal, kill, argue, cause division, and destroy, then you'd better enjoy it now, as your time is short.

You can be all religious, like the scribes and Pharisees, pretending to be an uppity, muckety-duck that's holier than everyone else. It's no skin off my nose what you decide to do. Everyone will pay the piper for what we owe. You can follow made-up traditions with oh-so-holy repetitions, long, drawn-out prayers, and meaningless rituals. But good luck with that. Traditions of men make the Word of God void.

"Making the word of God of none effect through your tradition, which ye have delivered: and many such like things do ye" (Mk 7:13).

Poppa only wants a humble, honest, pure, genuine, childlike love. His command is for us to love ourselves and others. He requires us to apologize when we mess up and to ask Him and others for forgiveness. He also commanded us to celebrate the Passover in remembrance that He — Jesus — died for us on that dark and dreary Passover Day — on that Old Rugged Cross. That's it! Easy Cheesy! No traditions of men necessary!

We should be patient and compassionate toward others who haven't yet learned how to command Satan out of their lives. With Jesus inside us, we have power over all our enemies, including Satan. When we have Jesus in our hearts as our protector, we can — in Jesus' name — command Satan and all evil spirits to get back to hell where they came from, never to return. There will always be another evil spirit trying tomorrow — so keep your bat handy. Practice makes perfect.

We can also command a gazillion times more pain, torment, and agony upon them. The other evil minions will see what happens to those who mess with us. They'll think twice before bothering us who have Jesus in our hearts. Evil spirits and even Satan will flee from us because we have the power to inflict them with immense pain and agony. They see we are unafraid to use this power! Jesus is the Master Goose who has the best juice!

Satan and his evil angels influence many people around us, including at work, with friends, spouses, and family members. He will use anyone who doesn't have the power of Jesus. If something feels loving, it's from our Poppa. However, if it makes us feel like using the sick bucket, then it's from Satan.

Satan's primary goal is to corrupt and destroy everyone's souls. Satan hates and wants to hurt our Poppa with all his heart, mind, strength, and spirit. There is a spiritual war going on, and Satan and his evil angels are working hard to cause confusion and division.

Our Poppa loves us all very much. It will be a sorrowful day for Him when He blots out His unloving children. We need to be just as diligent in working hard for Father. With all the pain Satan is inflicting upon His heart, let those of us who love Poppa shine brightly for Him. We must bring Him as much joy and happiness as possible. Let's strive to be perfect in love for Him and each other, because that brings our Poppa tremendous pleasure and enjoyment.

~ Goosebumps ~

Over the years, my mom and some of my siblings became more mean-spirited. A few years after I got a divorce, I got pregnant with a surprise baby. I called Mom to tell her she was a grandma again. We didn't talk often because she had shared my private information with Danielle, even after I asked her to keep it confidential. I realized I couldn't trust her, so I stopped calling her as much. Whenever I did, I always heard a bunch of judgmental and critical noises from her. I was tired of feeling those goosebumps.

When I called, she asked me many judgmental questions. She questioned whether I would get married and if I was living with the guy. During the call, she mentioned she wasn't doing very well. My sister Sadie's daughter, Amber, had moved far away to live with her dad. Mom said she felt depressed because she missed Amber. I told her I had an extra computer that she could have if she wanted it. I offered it so she could talk face-to-face with Amber. She said she would think about it.

Well, think about it — she did! It's more like she painted me as the villain who was forcing evil technology on her. The next time my brother Jesse visited her, boy oh boy, did she lay it on thick! I'm sure she first gossiped, judged, and criticized me for having a baby without being married. Then she exaggerated that I was forcing her to have an evil computer in her house!

I received a long, hurtful message from Jesse. He told me to stop forcing Mom to get a computer. He said that she doesn't want it and, besides, she wouldn't know how to use it anyway. Jesse ended his harsh message by telling me to keep myself and my illegitimate child in Minnesota, where we belong. Wow! Goosebumps rose on my skin as I felt my face go pale. I've done nothing harmful to Jesse. What a broken toaster! I didn't deserve his burnt toast! Many times, I've seen Mom act in a judgmental, critical, and gossipy manner. I know exactly how mean she was toward me behind my back. Jesse is co-dependent with her, so he felt the need to protect her from my evil computer and my "ungodly" devilish child, who was born out of wedlock.

In a calm message, I told Jesse that I wasn't forcing anything on Mom. I was only offering to help her have face-to-face communication with Amber. I told him I don't appreciate his judging me or calling my baby an illegitimate child. Then, I told him he should focus on his own mistakes instead of judging me and my life. I brought up his pornography, anger, and cruelty toward his kids. I ended by telling him I didn't want to hear from him again unless he learned how to be loving.

Codependency occurs when someone changes their behavior to seek approval from another person. Jesse is codependent with Mom. He never feels like he can be himself and fears that Mom will be judgmental and critical of him. Jesse believes he must impress her to be seen as her best kid. He would never dare disagree with anything she says. If she complains about someone, Jesse will also add that person to his naughty list.

Mom is a master manipulator. Behind their backs, she complains about one kid to the other. She shows disapproval of the kid she's talking about, to control the kid she's speaking to. She uses derogatory statements about people in the community to reprimand you. It's a passive-aggressive way of showing her disapproval of your behavior.

For example, a year after I had my little surprise baby, I was talking to Mom on the phone. In a condescending tone, she told me about a girl in her church who had gotten pregnant out of wedlock. I'm familiar with my mom's tactics, and I've learned how to deal with them. However, I still felt like she was using passive-aggressive tactics to shame me as she scorned that girl. The hair on the back of my neck stood up. I told her I also had become pregnant before marriage and am still not married — as if she didn't know! I said that these things happen to the best of us. I expressed my hope that people wouldn't judge that girl too harshly, since we all make mistakes. Then, I said, "Getting pregnant before marriage isn't any worse than gossiping."

Mom is a gossip, so I'm sure my comment gave her goosebumps. I was exposing her behavior to compare it to her view of premarital pregnancy. I was confident and assertive as I showed her she could no longer control or have power over me. She couldn't use her passive-aggressive scolding and criticism of others to belittle me. I no longer allow her to condemn me that way.

Jesse would never stand up to her. He would just take the beating and pretend he didn't feel wounded. He simply changes the subject and continues acting like he's her obedient little boy who still deserves his mother's scolding. If he dared to be himself, she might stop loving him. If he challenged her, she might gossip about him behind his back — not realizing that she already does. He doesn't yet have enough self-confidence or self-love. He's unable to embrace who he is and distance himself from everyone who harms him — including his mother. Jesse believes he must honor his mother, regardless of her behavior.

The difficulty in recognizing this type of manipulation lies in its passive-aggressive nature. It's hard to detect because it initially appears harmless or passive. However, in reality, it's an aggressive, judgmental, and critical remark that isn't directly aimed at you, but it is intended to condemn or control you. Sometimes, you're unsure whether they directed their comment at you. Your gut feels like they did, but you're not entirely sure.

You also can't fathom that your mother wants to manipulate and control your actions. At first, I thought Mom was just religious. I believed that made her derogatory statements acceptable. Mom also uses tears to emphasize her judgments and criticisms. Manipulative tears can also make passive-aggressive behavior hard to spot. I thought she was only sad. I didn't realize her tears came from a deep desire to control others.

Codependency formed early in us children. We were all molded and became little bumps on our mother goose. We were taught that it was our duty to please Mom. If we didn't, it meant we didn't love her. When Anna, Ella, and Jerry were young, Mom read them a poem about which child loved their mother the best. The poem ended by saying that the most helpful child was the one who loved her mother the most.

My mom read this poem to my siblings repeatedly to encourage them to be obedient and helpful. With each reading, she shaped them to be the child who pleased her the most. The rest of us kids never heard this poem, but we all became co-dependent on our mom. That poem somehow never left our home. Anna told me that just thinking about it still gives her goosebumps today.

As we grew into young adults, we all tried to please our mother the most. We didn't make decisions without wondering how Mom would feel about them. We never made mistakes without fearing Mom's judgment and criticism. We all wish we could receive her love for who we are, mistakes and all. Still, our mom doesn't want us to make mistakes, so she uses her learned passive-aggressive, judgmental, critical, and manipulative techniques to make us perfect children. When one of us doesn't bend to her will, she abandons us as the unruly child, the black sheep.

It's impossible to buy Mom's love. Many of us have tried. I've given her money, bought her vitamins, probiotics, a back massager, a zapper, a toxin foot bath, and similar gifts. She never remembers these presents. Our worthiness of her love depends on whether we attend her church and follow its doctrine.

I offered her a place to live with me when she can no longer care for herself. Instead of thanking me for the offer, she turned up her nose, saying that living with me would cause her too much depression. I know she was implying that she would become depressed because I have a television, wear pants, and don't believe in her church's teachings. Her church doesn't allow her to have a TV or wear pants. She was putting me down instead of showing gratitude, so I guess she'll end up in a nursing home. Guess what? There's a TV there too; the nurses wear pants; and most of them don't share her beliefs.

Caring for her would have been difficult. But I felt that, as her daughter, it was my duty to offer. I believe differently from her, and with all her judgment and criticism, she would be a handful. Also, I moved 10 hours away for a reason. I did my part by making the offer, and since she was ungrateful in rejecting it, I won't make another one. Unless she becomes homeless and lives on the streets, the nursing home is the best place for her.

~ Birds of a Feather ~

Some of my sisters still have a co-dependent relationship with Mom. As adults, they either continue to attend her church or remain heavily influenced by its teachings. They also share her judgment and criticism toward me and others who don't believe in their strict predestination-only and no-free-will religious beliefs.

A few years ago, Mom had a stroke and almost died. Sadie started a group chat with all the siblings. The chat was going well, but when I mentioned going to heaven, Sadie, Jolene, and Susan became hostile toward me.

Sadie and her husband, Jason, had made some hurtful jabs at me in the past. I already stopped talking to Sadie after realizing she and Jason are malicious people. Sadie added the whole family to the group chat. It's no surprise that things didn't go well. They have become cruel because of their religious hierarchy. Here's where things started going sour:

Jolene: *Thx, Sadie. Must fight mom with the other stuff that she takes (vitamins) & whatnot. Makes her nuts!*

Sadie: *I went through meds yesterday & put out of sight, out of mind all the bottles of crap she doesn't take anyway.*

Me: *Has anyone else considered Mom to be "nuts" because of taking vitamins?*

Susan: *No, why would she be?*

Me: *I'm just making sure that I'm not missing something.*

Jolene: *Ok, Olivia... figure of speech! Cool it! Sheesh!*

Me: *Oh. I thought you were being serious, that Mom acts "nuts" because of her daily vitamins. I apologize for misunderstanding your post.*

Jolene: *The antibiotic is making her nuts! Never meant she was at all! People who see her regularly know that.*

Me: *I know I live 10 hours away and can't see her regularly. I know we have life after death. I can sit around enjoying a glass of wine with her then.*

Sadie: *Let's hope so. Make our calling and election sure; God will not be mocked.*

Jolene: *Last thing Ma would want!*

Susan: *That's my thoughts too, Sadie.*

Me: *If anyone thought I was mocking God, I wasn't doing that. Please don't be hateful toward me for a simple wine statement. Jesus turned the water into wine, so it must be fine. John Calvin, the founder of Calvinism, also regularly drank wine.*

The chat ended. Over the next few days, I realized Sadie had started a different chat. I had stopped receiving updates on Mom's condition. When I talked to Anna a few days later, she confirmed my suspicions. Sadie began her new group chat by saying, "This is a new chat, with Olivia expelled." I approached Sadie about her hurtful behavior toward me.

Me: *You have deleted me from the family group chat.*

Sadie: *I don't stand for narcissistic abuse; therefore, I did what was best for me. I know you'll understand.*

Me: *Please don't contact me again. You are not my sister. Lose my number. Seriously.*

The chat ended. Sadie had now struck out. She had hurt me many times before. Because she was a blood relative, I gave her more chances than I should have before cutting tics with her. I didn't leave the door open for her to return. She will always act viciously and hatefully toward anyone who believes in free will.

Sadie's church doesn't allow her to love herself, so she will never learn how to love others. They teach her she can't love God. They tell her she's not worthy of God's love. As a result, she will always feel deep-seated worthlessness and struggle with low self-esteem. These negative feelings about herself spill over toward others as hateful, critical, vicious, and judgmental backbiting and gossiping.

Her church teaches her she's special because it claims to have "God's only truth." This sense of being special gives Sadie a feeling of religious superiority over others. She believes that being mean to me is her God-given right because she sees me as an unsaved Gentile destined for hell.

In reflection, I initially thought Sadie believed I was mocking God when I joked about enjoying a glass of wine with Mom in heaven. As I reflected further, I remembered she believes in a predestination-only and no-free-will doctrine. Sadie actually implied that I mocked God because I assumed I would be in heaven.

She said, "Make our election and calling sure," as a warning to me. She was implying I should not assume that I will be in heaven. Since I'm not a member of her church, to her, I was mocking God by saying I'm going to heaven.

Her church stole from Sadie her love of God, love for herself, and her love for others. They also reject faith and works. Instead, they emphasize a hellfire-and-damnation approach. They don't teach that Jesus died on the cross for whosoever will.

Sadie believes that a person who loves themself is a narcissist, which is why she called me a narcissist. She views someone who is assertive and stands up for themselves as bossy.

Sadie, Jolene, and Susan are vultures who thrive by feeding on each other's negativity as they stab their beaks into the hearts of others. Birds of a feather flock together.

~ House of Cards ~

A couple of years later, my oldest brother, Jerry, had a heart attack, or a card-iac arrest. The ambulance rushed him to the hospital. The doctors performed several surgeries, tried to save his life, and placed him on life support. He was 63 years old. Unfortunately, he didn't survive. Because of factors such as time, work, distance, children, and family dysfunction, I wasn't close to Jerry or his wife, Darcy. I didn't know either of them well.

Jerry and his wife, Darcy, were the primary caregivers for their nine grandchildren. Darcy's daughter had lost her home because of severe flooding six months earlier. She was struggling to find a new place and get back on her feet. For many years, Jerry worked as a farmhand for a local farmer. He received free housing in one of the farmer's spare homes and extra pay. Darcy did not work outside the home; she stayed home to care for the children. Jerry and Darcy were poor and did not have health or life insurance.

Sadie once again started a family group chat that included all the siblings and Jerry's wife, Darcy. Considering our family's dysfunction, the conversation began well, but, as usual, it didn't end well. Broken trust and unkind behavior have damaged our family as a whole.

To provide some background about Sadie, our mom has reported Sadie and Jason to Child Protective Services twice because of severe bruises on their children. Verbal and physical abuse have become common in their household. Both Sadie and Jason were victims of abuse during their childhoods. As they grew into adults, they married and continued the vicious cycle, becoming abusers themselves toward their children and others.

As the group chat shows, because of their extreme religious beliefs, Sadie, Jolene, and Susan once again directed their hateful and disrespectful verbal abuse toward me.

Within the chat, I let Sadie freely express her hostility toward me. I hoped the other family members would see her abusive nature. Part of me also wanted to show my siblings how to stand up to her and give them hope that they, too, could someday escape her toxic behavior.

Escaping from abusive people can be difficult until they reveal their cards. I let Sadie show her full hand. All she had was a pair of jokers — filled with satanic, abusive, and vicious behavior. While Sadie isn't the only one who is cruel, she is the most vicious.

December 24

Sadie: *Good morning. Just got off the phone with Darcy. Jerry is at the heart hospital. They will transfer him to the regular hospital sometime today. He has several spots on his brain that don't look good (hematomas). The doctor said we need a miracle.*

Ben: *He passed away. Emma just finished talking to James. She told him that Jerry had passed away.*

Darcy: *No, they're transferring him. Who am I talking to?*

Sadie: *Thanks, Darcy. These are all the brothers and sisters. Share with us what you know. Any more information updates?*

Darcy: *It isn't good news. The brain doctor is coming in to talk to us. From what they are telling me, he'll have to be removed from life support. The doctor is supposed to be here by 5:00. Visit now if you want to say goodbye.*

Anna: *Our prayers are with you, Darcy, and your family.*

Harlan: *Prayers for our whole family in this difficult time.*

Me: *My condolences to us all as well. I'm sorry to hear this sad news. What can we do to help you, Darcy?*

Danielle: *Mom, Sadie, Glen, and I are at the hospital right now. Darcy will wait a bit if there's anyone who would like to come. If you know you are coming, please send a text back to let us know. His brain is swelling, and his temperature keeps rising. The nurse said he won't last long when she takes him off the machine. But Darcy encourages anyone to come. She'll wait if you want to visit.*

December 25

Harlan: *Came to see Jerry this morning. Had a nice chat with the nurse. She said they are thinking of taking him off life support. They will do organ donation either Thursday or Friday.*

Me: *Thanks for the updates. Please let me know if there's anything I can do to help Darcy and the children.*

Darcy: *Okay.*

Ella: *Hi, Olivia. This is Ella. You are so dear! Love you! That goes for everyone else, too! God be with you all during this time and always. Take care and Merry Christmas, if that's possible.*

Me: *(Sent hearts)*

Ella: *Back at ya!*

Me: *(I sent a virtual Christmas card picture with Jesus in the manger that said Happy Birthday Jesus. Merry Christmas, everyone.)*

Ella: *You bet. It's the only reason for the season, isn't it? If we know Christ and are saved, we are most blessed indeed!*

Me: *Yes. He is a very loving Poppa. Best ever!*

Side note: Ella isn't a member of Mom's church and has built a relationship with our Heavenly Father. She and I were the only ones to say Merry Christmas. Because of their religious beliefs, my family doesn't wish each other Merry Christmas, but I took a gamble on saying it in the chat anyway.

Jolene: *Thanks so much for the update. Take care, everyone.*

Darcy: *Will do. You are welcome.*

December 26

Susan: *Emma said she's coming up today and wants to make sure they wait to take him off life support until she can say goodbye to him.*

Jesse: *Still at the heart hospital?*

Sadie: *Yes.*

Darcy: *They aren't doing anything with him until 10:00 tomorrow morning.*

Darcy: *Whoever is visiting him, he's no longer on any pain medicine, so hopefully you all have respect to be quiet and not rile him up. Thank you.*

Side note: Darcy felt anxious that people would talk too loudly at Jerry's bedside. Many of them haven't learned social etiquette. Her making this statement caused them to lose sympathy for her. How dare she tell them to show respect?

December 27

Darcy: *Jerry passed peacefully at 11:59. His eyes and tissue were able to be donated. God bless his soul.*

Ella: *Thoughts and prayers are with you, Darcy.*

Me: *Ecclesiastes 12:7 Then shall the dust return to the earth as it was: and the spirit shall return unto God who gave it. A sad day for us, but a joyful day for Jerry to be back home with our Heavenly Father.*

Harlan: *May the Lord uphold and strengthen each of us today and in the days to come.*

Susan: *(Put a heart by Harlan's post)*

Side note: Susan put a heart next to Harlan's religious post to show her appreciation for his comment. Harlan attends her church. However, she didn't heart my scripture post about Jerry being in heaven because she doesn't believe he went there. Jerry wasn't a member of her church. Susan's church teaches that God's elect — His saved people — will only be found within her specific church. She believes her church is God's only truth. She thinks she holds all the cards. If someone doesn't follow her doctrine, then they are not one of God's chosen. Therefore, they won't go to heaven.

Sadie: *If anyone wants to be part of the funeral plans, contact Darcy's sister-in-law, Jane.*

Alex: *When is the funeral? Visitation on Monday, funeral on Tuesday? You can let me know. Thanks.*

Darcy: *Just to let everybody know, I will be meeting with the funeral director. Whoever would like to show up and have a part in this, it's 5:00 tomorrow.*

Harlan: *Thanks, Darcy. We'll be there at 5:00.*

Me: *I can join via FaceTime if you'd like. The funeral home will explain the costs of a casket versus cremation, and I can share my thoughts here. The expense is significantly lower for cremation, as there are no funeral home fees, cemetery costs, visitation, church service, or luncheon expenses. I have an unused urn here that we can use if you decide cremation is an option for you. Funeral homes make bank from selling urns and caskets.*

I've told my kids, "Here's the urn. Pick out a small tree and have a nice planting service at home for me. Plant my ashes under the new little tree in the backyard. Have a little family get-together at the house, cook food, sing songs, share thanks, and reminisce." Cremation and keeping the cost as low as possible is my recommendation, but if someone can afford the more expensive casket option, that's fine as well.

Side note: I'm sure my recommendation shocked and outraged some of my family. I bet their eyes almost popped out of their sockets because I had the nerve to suggest cremation. Behind my back, I'm sure they panicked, texting and calling each other in disbelief and expressing their disdain for me and my cremation idea. Only their gentle sister, Olivia, would dare to suggest doing such a terrible thing!

After the funeral meeting:

Harlan: *Tuesday is the funeral. The family will be at the funeral home at noon to view the body — public viewing from 1 to 2, and service at 2:30 in the chapel.*

Jolene: *Thank you, Harlan, for your help with the hard decisions and for letting us all know about the plans that were made.*

Harlan: *You're welcome. It was a group decision.*

Jolene: *Good. Love to all our family.*

Susan: *Love you too.*

Danielle: *Thank you.*

Sadie: *I hope the weather holds out!*

Side note: They are all thankful to have received the casket.

December 29

Sadie: *(Posted a picture of the obituary).*

Harlan: *Nice, thanks!*

December 30

Me: *With the weather, roads, and freezing temperatures, it's safer and wiser not to travel. My vehicle has been acting up lately, and there's too much risk of it breaking down halfway there or back, especially since no mechanic will be available because of the holidays. I'll have a private goodbye here at home for Jerry. I've been thinking about getting a black cherry tree and planting it this spring in remembrance of Jerry.*

Side note: I'm sure most of them were relieved I wouldn't be coming. Now they wouldn't have to be around their free-willed, gentle sister, who suggested cremation and believes Jerry is in heaven. I was also relieved. It wouldn't have been easy to be around most of them.

Susan: *I have had a large hosta for many years in memory of Pete.*

Me: *That's nice, Susan. They are beautiful.*

Darcy: *Ok*

Sadie: *(Sent a picture of Jerry and Pete at Jerry and Darcy's wedding)*

Sadie: *Cheers!*

Alex: *Nice picture.*

Darcy: *Together again.*

Jolene: *Definitely a keeper!*

Alex: *Right. I like it.*

Darcy: *Thank you all for being there for me at this time. God bless you guys.*

Jolene: *We Love You!*

Alex: *Love you all, too.*

December 31 (Funeral Day)

Danielle: *(Sent picture of Jerry as a toddler)*

Danielle: *So many people who came through the line today expressed how Jerry always had a smile, was kind, and was a hard worker. Many of his co-workers came, and we commented on how nice that was! You could tell he meant a lot to them. Thank you to the siblings who came. And it was so nice to see many of your children there as well. Take care, Darcy. Thinking of you and praying for you in the days ahead.*

Side note: Danielle's excessive pointing out and praising of how many of Jerry's co-workers attended the funeral, along with thanking those who showed up, was nothing less than passive-aggressive behavior meant to guilt and shame the siblings who didn't attend.

January 1

Me: *I spoke with Darcy to find out how we can help her and the children. Food is something they need. Can each family prepare 5-10 different casseroles in disposable aluminum 9x13 pans with contents and cooking instructions written on the lid? Freeze them in your freezer, and we can arrange a pickup day. If you bring them to the pickup person, they can take them to Darcy. If the cost of ingredients would cause you financial hardship, I can provide a $10 reimbursement for each casserole you make for her. It would be great to have these made and delivered to her by next weekend. Please let me know with a yes or no if you can help.*

January 2

Sadie: *Yes. Any allergies?*

Anna: *I'll send a grocery gift card.*

Me: *Does anyone have a freezer or know someone who has extra space to store casseroles until we can deliver them? Can anyone pick up the casseroles and bring them to Darcy?*

Side note: I received two responses from people who said they'd help. The rest ignored me because I recommended cremation, said Jerry was in heaven, and I didn't attend his funeral. Danielle and I had not spoken for 12 ½ years, so no surprise.

Me: *Darcy's situation is more urgent than just needing food, and if anyone can help her financially, she desperately* *needs it. She hasn't been working outside the home as she is raising the nine children. She has no source of income. Jerry was the sole source of the family's income.*

As part of Jerry's income, they live in the hired-hand house. Darcy will have to move out soon. She could get a job, but the cost of daycare for nine children would be more than her earnings.

Hopefully, she can get Jerry's Social Security if the farmer paid that in. That's all down the road a bit. Death certificates take a few weeks to get. Getting all the documents can take several months.

The hospital called and informed her that Jerry's bill is $287,000.

Coffin, cemetery plot, vault, ceremonies, luncheon, etc., also fall on Darcy's shoulders. Darcy's brother paid for the funeral, but it was a loan to her. She now owes her brother $12,500. At the funeral, Darcy received $800 through cards. That's only a small part of the huge cost of an elaborate funeral. If you voted for the expensive casket, will you please help her pay that enormous debt?

Darcy and the children need a place to stay. I offer my home to them all for as long as they need support. I understand this is a lot, but please consider helping our sister Darcy and her children if you can.

1 John 3:17 "But whoso hath this world's good, and seeth his brother have need, and shutteth up his bowels of compassion from him, how dwelleth the love of God in him?"

Side note: I was feeling quite upset that they all voted for and demanded the expensive casket funeral. When it came down to the wire, they didn't chip in with the money to help pay for it. They left Darcy holding the bag.

Ben: *With no herd bumper*

Sadie: *What's a herd bumper? Sorry, I'm lost....*

Ben: *Wrong recipient*

Ella: *I have a lot of boxed and canned food. I'll give and trust the Lord to provide for us if times get tough. It would be great if someone could use this food now, as it will expire. I can bring it to her. That wouldn't be a problem. What do you think? I just don't have time to make casseroles (excellent idea though)! Love, love, love you all! Thanks, everyone, for all you've done to help during this time of need.*

Me: *Ben.... Herd bumper = Life insurance? Yes. No herd bumper.*

Side note: Many of my family members don't believe in life insurance.

Me: *Ella, Darcy has to vacate that house in the coming months, so not too much until she gets settled into another place. I'm sure that while Darcy is grieving the loss of her husband and breadwinner, it's tough to find the energy to* *cook. Pre-made casseroles will help her. However, please bring her some of what you have now and some more later. Keep some for yourself as well. It's always good to have some extra supplies on hand in case of an emergency. Will you please also bring the casseroles to her when you bring your box of goodies?*

Me: *Sadie, thank you for making casseroles. Do you have a freezer that can hold everyone's casseroles? A drop-off spot would help store them until we make the delivery. Does Mom have a big freezer we can use?*

Anna, thanks for sending Darcy a food card. That will be very helpful. Do we have anyone else who can make casseroles for Darcy?

Ben: *Olivia, hun, I sent herd bumper by accident, but that's a pretty neat way to describe life insurance.*

Sadie: *Olivia, hun. When do you plan to come and help assemble these casseroles? My kitchen is open. I just have no freezer space.*

Side note: Sadie's mocking of Ben's use of "hun" was my first clue that she was acting viciously behind the scenes. With me living 10 hours away, she knew I wasn't making casseroles. However, I was trying to organize a much-needed food drive and would pay out-of-pocket if someone were to cook, freeze, and deliver meals to Darcy and her nine children. I laughed it off and kept the conversation light to see if I was misreading her.

Me: *Lol. It would be better for me to stay here and work to help Darcy with cold, hard cash. If you're short on money, I'll pay $10 for every casserole anyone makes for her. Share your pictures of each casserole before you put the lid on it.*

Susan: *Olivia, I've had enough. People don't tell others what to give. Enough already. You put your opinions here, so there's mine!*

Side note: Nope, I wasn't misreading anything. This was Susan's retaliation against me for sharing my "heretical" cremation opinions, which had upset her very much.

Me: *A simple no is sufficient if you don't want to or can't participate in the food drive for Darcy.*

Sadie: *I second the motion. I don't know how to delete people from the group, so bye bye.*

Me: *What exactly is going on? Second what motion? Delete who from the group?*

(1½ hours later).

Me: *Sigh. Are people being hateful and cruel again? I'm sorry that some of you are choosing those behaviors again.*

Jolene: *Time's up! After 9 pm.*

Side note: It has always been in their cards for them to be cruel. My strong suit is being able to call a spade a spade. It was time for me to show my hand and lay my cards on the table. They had now raised the stakes with their hatred and cruelty. If I played my cards right, I could show some of them the difference between loving and unloving behavior. My wild card of love might win a few of them over to our Poppa's side of the fence.

January 3

Me: *Unloving (of Satan) behavior includes: Gossiping- talking about others behind their backs — Backbiting- pretending to be a friend, then stabbing them in the back — Judgmental- hell to all others for their mistakes — Condescending- looking down your noses at others — Critical- nitpicking other people, their lives, and their decisions — Name-calling- bastard child and narcissist fall under this category — Haughty- better-than-thou — Religious hierarchy- belief that all others who don't go to your church are gentiles and going to hell — Unloving- hateful, vicious, cruel — Unforgiving- holds a grudge for years — Don't give a hoot- having a negative attitude toward others — Pretend Christian- say they are Christian, but then do all the above behaviors.*

Loving (of God) behavior includes: Kindness; Gentleness; Helpfulness; Genuine love; Patience; Understanding; Compassion; Non-judgmental; Humble; Forgiving; Not gossiping. If any of the above unloving behaviors were in heaven, I'd never want to go there. People who exhibited those behaviors killed Jesus.

Sadie: *Olivia. We've had enough! I am all the things above, and you are as well. No one is excluded. Block me from your phone if you want to. I don't care.*

Side note: Sadie doesn't want to hear about her unloving behavior. It shocked me to hear her admit she engages in those unloving actions. However, I was even more surprised when she said she believes everyone's behavior is like hers. This helps me understand the old saying that people judge others by the coin in their own pocket.

Sadie: *And besides that, there are no casseroles or money or time going Darcy's direction. You have ruined that for her, so you know!*

Side note: Hmm. No dice for Darcy. Didn't Susan, Sadie, and Jolene start this cruel and hateful behavior? I wanted to organize a food drive for Darcy, who just lost her husband and now has nine children to feed. My punishment for calling Sadie out on her cruelty toward me is that now none of them will help Darcy.

Sadie: *We don't need to be bossed around by some narcissistic sister who always has to have the last word! Tired of it. Let us grieve in peace without shoving anything else down our throats! I feel I have spoken for the whole group here, because I received many phone calls yesterday saying such. Enough!*

Side note: They see my attempt to organize a food drive as bossy. Unaware that Jesus said to love our neighbor as ourselves, Sadie believes anyone who loves themselves is a narcissist. Her church teaches her not to love herself. They say self-love is prideful, and pride is a sin. Her religious hierarchy and name-calling stem from her biblical illiteracy.

Me: *Matthew 25:40 And the King shall answer and say unto them, Verily I say unto you, Inasmuch as ye have done it unto one of the least of these my brethren, ye have done it unto me.*

Susan: *Why do you bring church into things? I wish you had heard the thought-provoking funeral message! It was that there might not be another day for us. We are to prepare today, for tomorrow isn't promised, as we saw (again). James 4 was the passage.*

Side note: Susan wished I could have heard her preacher's sermon at the funeral. Her preacher is hypocritical in his preaching. Prepare today? For tomorrow we may die? Come on, Susan. Really? Her church teaches that we can't do anything to be saved. Which one is it? Nothing you can do — or prepare today?

Me: *The church's messages should teach us how to love our Heavenly Father and our neighbors as ourselves. If they don't, they aren't teaching what Jesus taught. I include the church because Jesus and those who love Him are the church. Jesus is all there is — He is everything. He is the only way to receive eternal life. John 14:15: If ye love me, keep my commandments.*

Sadie: *Susan. There is much "Religion" that never comes to fruition.*

Side note: Sadie is telling Susan that my belief in loving Father, loving ourselves, and loving others is just another religion that never bears fruit. Her church teaches that all other religions are false. Sadie's definition of "fruition" is that a saved person will realize they are a worthless piece of garbage and unworthy of Poppa's love. Once they realize this, they'll remain in self-hatred for the rest of their lives.

Susan: *It's sad that I haven't read anything in your words about our state as sinners before the Savior. A lot of people these days don't need that. They're saved already. That's the mistake.*

Side note: Susan is talking about her belief that God's predestined saved people will enter a state of feeling worthless and unworthy of God's love. To them, salvation isn't real unless a person continuously wallows in hate, sorrow, guilt, and shame toward themselves for the rest of their lives.

Me: *Of course, we all sin. But when we ask Jesus to come into our hearts to lead and guide us, and when we repent and feel sorry for how we've treated others, then we change our behavior to please our Heavenly Father. Father forgives us when our hearts cry out to Him with sincere sorrow for our past wrongs. We ask Him to help us do what is right and to stop acting unloving. We turn ourselves over to Him as worthy servants, and we help Him pull as many of His children as possible out of Satan's grasp.*

Sadie: *A foot too high. He that heareth let him understand.*

Side note: Sadie, using passive-aggressive Bible code to her besties, implied that I think too highly of myself. Becoming a servant for our Poppa is unfamiliar to her, and she perceives me as claiming something I'm not allowed to. She believes we can't surrender our hearts to our Poppa or invite Jesus into our hearts. Sadie doesn't believe we have the free will to choose to love our Poppa, which is why she shows religious hostility toward me here. When I explained the basic process of how to be saved, it triggered Sadie, and she started spewing her religious hierarchy hatred and judgment toward me. All bets were off for her. She was going for the throat.

Me: *I hear you, Sadie, and I understand. Please stop acting vicious toward me. Our Heavenly Father doesn't appreciate you doing that. I am the apple of His eye because I love Him very much. If you poke me, you are poking our Poppa in the eye. I don't recommend that.*

Sadie: *Excuse me!? I'm not taking that! I will not be pushed around by someone who always has to have the last word and thinks she knows everything. I just poked you. Sorry, not sorry. Get out of this group and do the rest of us a favor! You have officially pushed my very last button, and I am not taking it anymore! By the way...*

Have you forgiven Jason for stopping by Danielle's house "on purpose" because he knew you hated her and you didn't want to see her!? Have you forgiven Peggy for whatever she did to you, and ghosted her!? It sounds like you have not forgiven me for whatever I did to you!? So it looks to me like let's take the mote out of our own eye before we can take the beam out of our brother's eye! There is no time or place *for all of this BS. I will not let you ruin my day, or have that power over me! I love you from a distance, and I still say you're my sister, but this behavior has to stop. PLEASE get yourself checked out, Olivia. This is what I am hearing from the rest of the group: there's something a little off in your head! There, I told it to your face. I didn't tell anyone else this, but they can read it right in this text. Get a day job! I'm tired of my phone dinging with your b*llsh*t!*

Side note: When you ask an abusive person to please stop being vicious to you, they will often go into full demon mode. They'll try to gaslight you and claim that you are the problem. When I asked Sadie to stop being cruel to me, she said I was pushing her around and abusing her. What turned Sadie into a demon was when I said I'm the apple of my Heavenly Father's eye, and I love Him very much. All bets were off for her. She went into full-blown religious hierarchy attack mode and wanted to knock me back down to size. To her, nobody can choose to love our Poppa.

Ben: *Is it a Herd Bumper?*

Ben: *Oh, sorry, wrong person.*

Side note: Too funny. Ben also had his bargaining chip on the table while trying to buy some farm equipment. He kept texting the wrong message by mistake. It was a good time to collapse the house of cards and reveal some of the bad hands my abusive family members had dealt me. I put on my poker face and shuffled the cards — let the chips fall where they may.

Me: *I'll try to explain. I don't hate Danielle. That's not true. I'll tell you the story.*

Through gossip, Danielle had heard that I was thinking about getting a divorce. Danielle attacked me with criticism and judgment at Hannah's graduation party. She believed it was her religious duty to tell me I was going to hell if I divorced. She said God expected me to stay married and work it out no matter what. I tried to explain my broken heart to her and that I just couldn't handle his lying, stealing, and porn anymore.

Danielle showed me no compassion. Her only concern was to cast hellfire and damnation upon me. Danielle wouldn't back down, so after half an hour of trying to persuade me not to commit such a terrible sin, I asked her to mind her own business. I told her I needed to do what was right for me. This didn't end well, as she said in a haughty tone that she would pray for me.

I yelled at her, "That's judging!" I walked away. I went back to the party, which was now ruined because of her religious beliefs and unloving behavior. She went crying to the family members at the party, and now I'm the villain. She left without saying goodbye.

I called her about a year later. I told her we are sisters, and having this rift between us isn't good. I apologized for my part in what happened. She said, "You told me to mind my own business." I chuckled a bit and said, "Well, if we had that same conversation today, I'd still ask you to mind your own business. But I'd be calmer and more patient." She said, "Well, I guess that's how it is then." I said, "Okay, well, I love you." We both said goodbye without her forgiving me for getting angry at her. She didn't apologize for minding my business and throwing all her hellfire and damnation at me. We haven't spoken for 12 ½ years.

Jason knew this situation when he stopped by their house after we all went out to eat. I felt he did it on purpose because he loves to stir the pot. Jason, if you didn't do this on purpose, I apologize for saying that in confidence to someone I thought was a trusted friend.

Side note: When my chips were down, Danielle showed no compassion. She kicked me while I was down and turned my already broken heart into a shattered one. We can call her the Queen of Hearts.

Me: *I'll try to explain the next attack.*

I had been texting Peggy every day for a few years, every morning and throughout the day. I felt we were friends, and we shared our lives. One night, Ben stopped by for a visit while traveling through my area. The next morning, I saw a message from Peggy saying, "I heard you had a visitor last night." I replied to Peggy, asking, "How did you know about that?"

Peggy ignored me for a full day and a half without replying. It was unusual because we always said good morning and chatted throughout the day. I figured out that it was because she was gossiping with Sadie. So, I grabbed my handy text machine and sent a serious message to Sadie, Peggy, and Ben's wife about the harmful effects of gossip and how it hurts people.

The result was that I asked Peggy for an apology for ignoring me, but she refused to apologize. I love Peggy, just as I love all of you, but when we hurt others, we need to apologize. I want to apologize to each of you if I have ever hurt you. Please bring it up here, and I will give you a sincere apology.

Peggy: *To set the record straight, and the truth, I apologized to you Olivia, numerous times, but you never accepted my apology because I never apologized to you "correctly" and it was not good enough for you, so you sent me a book of how I was supposed to apologize correctly to you, etc. so stop the nonsense — end of story and your bs lies. I went to gotoverit.org long ago.*

Side note: This is Peggy's first message in the group chat. I forced her hand and woke up the elephant under the rug. She wanted to follow suit and be dealt in as well. Peggy still hasn't apologized to me, and I doubt she ever will. Maybe at the Pearly Gates. No problem. I'm a patient person.

Ella: *Praying for you, Peggy, and hoping the pain isn't bothering you today. I love you.*

Side note: It sounds like Peggy might cash in her chips soon to arrive at the Heavenly Gates.

Sadie: *Let's hear about YOU.*

Sadie: *We all suck except you. Point taken. Have a good day!*

Side note: Sadie tried to deflect by using a sleight of hand, hoping to avoid discussing her abusive behavior. An abuser always tries to redirect attention to others. They never accept responsibility for their harmful actions. Instead, they blame you or say you're just as bad. They attempt to make it seem like you're the one at fault. Sadie didn't have an ace up her sleeve. She knows I'm not hateful or unloving toward others. She had already played her best card, and if she had any other tricks, she would have put her cards on the table. Sadie didn't like being called out for her destructive behavior. She desperately wanted to change the subject and shift the focus back to me.

Me: *I'm glad we can work through these traumas and heal some of our pain. Peggy, first off, I love you. I felt betrayed by your gossiping with Sadie behind my back. I felt you were ignoring me to avoid giving up Sadie as your source of gossip. When I told you I was hurting and needed an apology from you, you said you were sorry for my pain. Telling someone we're sorry for their pain is very different from apologizing for the pain we caused them. Yes, Peggy, I asked you to give me a genuine apology for participating in the gossip and ignoring me.*

I love you all. Our Heavenly Father loves us all very much. He wants us all to be loving and kind to each other. Was this gossip taught to us at home, school, church, or in our community? How did this verbal hurting of others take root in our family?

Sadie: *I genuinely LOVE Peggy and would NEVER cause her such needless pain! If you think we gossip about you, you're wrong. We don't waste our time with needless bull.*

The fact is, it doesn't even show up on the radar. Sorry to everyone who has had to put up with all this during WORK hours. Please delete the group as it's no longer useful.

This concludes the message. It was time to cash in my chips. As a servant of our Heavenly Father, I did my best to show His love to them. I also tried to shed light on some elephants shoved under the rug that destroyed our family.

~ Cards on the Table ~

Looking back, saying Merry Christmas to my family was strike one for me right from the start. They aren't keen on wishing others Christmas cheer. They don't believe we should feel joy about Jesus being born to pay the price for anyone who loves Him. Instead, they think Jesus was born only for a few chosen, predestined people.

Their Christmas church service is a solemn gathering focused on sin, shame, and unworthiness. Most families in the church gather at Christmas to share a large meal. None of them has a tree or decorations, and nobody exchanges gifts. They believe these traditions are only for the Gentiles destined for hell. Most hold a negative view of Christmas cards, especially those depicting Jesus in the manger. They see any inaccurate representation of Jesus as mocking God. For them, there's nothing merry about Christmas.

Many of my family members are staunch believers in John Calvin's predestination-only doctrine. They believe that before creating the earth or any people whatsoever, God watched a fast-forward video of sorts in His mind and foresaw the entirety of everyone's future actions, words, and thoughts. Then, based on this foresight, God predestined each person's ultimate destiny to either heaven or hell.

John Calvin taught that only a few people would enter heaven. In contrast, he said that God will cast the vast majority of billions of people into hell to suffer eternal, never-ending torment. He said, despite God's knowledge that most people's destination is hell, He created them all anyway. According to Calvin, no one has free will. Each person must live out the exact life and destiny that God has predetermined for them.

My family, followers of Calvin, believe that God is sitting atop His throne, watching a live-streaming, play-by-play, real-life version unfold. My family would bet the farm that John Calvin's predestination-only theory is God's only truth and the only game in town.

Strike two hit me when I called our Heavenly Father 'Poppa.' They saw this as disrespectful and irreverent. They overlook the fact that the Bible teaches us we must become like little children to enter the kingdom of heaven. Their teaching doesn't include embracing the Poppa-child concept, so they don't understand the beauty of having that kind of relationship with our Father.

Although Hebrews 4:16 encourages us to approach our Father's throne boldly, my family believes they must pray with deep reverence. Their faces look bleak and fearful, thinking they are never worthy of approaching Him. They visualize God as a stern, unforgiving, unloving, and wrathful figure, sitting far away in the heavens on a massive throne. They see Him as judgmental, angry, critical, unreachable, and unapproachable. It is unfamiliar to them that Poppa is loving, patient, understanding, compassionate, and forgiving.

By saying Jerry was in heaven, I definitely landed myself strike three. Jerry didn't attend their church, so how dare I say our brother entered the Pearly Gates! When I said this, I'm sure their eyes narrowed, their chests puffed out, and they all took sharp, deep, judgmental breaths. I envision their fists clenching, their nostrils flaring, and their jaws tightening as they struggle to contain their anger. This "gentile, fake, holy roller, free-willer" sister daring to claim Jerry's spirit went to heaven was just too much for them. I picture the smoke rolling from their ears as snide comments and backstabbing began — in a separate group message, of course, among themselves.

I'm sure I received my fourth strike, and I'm certain some of them went through the roof in disbelief that I recommended cremation. John Calvin taught that when Jesus returns at His second coming, all souls will re-enter their dead, rotted flesh bodies, and all flesh will rise from the graves. Since they believe we'll need our flesh bodies again, they oppose cremating the body. To them, cremation is a sin.

They must not realize that John Calvin handed Michael Servetus over to the authorities. They burned Michael at the stake with green wood, which caused him a slow and painful cremation. But I guess Michael won't need his body when Jesus returns?

Darcy's sister-in-law, Jane, called me to join the funeral meeting. I asked the funeral director about the prices for a burial with a casket and ceremonies versus cremation. He said that the total for the casket and services was $15,000. The cremation cost was $3700. When he asked which option they preferred, Mom, Harlan, Alex, and Jesse all said they wanted the casket.

I asked if anyone had money for the coffin so Darcy wouldn't become burdened. Jane and her husband said they could pay $2500 of the cost. No one else chipped in any money from their wallets to help pay for the funeral, despite their religious votes in favor of choosing the more expensive casket. I asked again how we could cover the cost. I was hoping they would put their money where their mouth is.

The phone call sounded muffled, but someone stepped up and offered to cover the rest, as I understood it. I didn't know who it was, but I thanked them for doing that. What a relief — or so I thought.

And, strike five. The funeral director asked what songs we wanted to sing at the funeral. I, their gentile sister, had the nerve to recommend "Amazing Grace" and "The Old Rugged Cross." With disdain in her voice, Mom dismissed my suggestions by saying, "We don't sing those songs in our church." When it was time to choose a poem or a Bible verse to include on the funeral bulletin, I mentioned that I had a couple of ideas if they needed options. They replied that they didn't need other options and would figure something out.

I'm sure after my "sinful cremation" and "unholy song" recommendations, many family members were vigorously shaking their heads "no" to Jane. They feared I would also offer them some "ungodly" Bible verses. Jane told me they didn't need any other options. I could tell from her tentative voice that something was going on behind the scenes. I'm certain they were acting apprehensive and wringing their hands vigorously.

Strike six occurred when I decided not to attend the funeral. Danielle complimented Jerry's coworkers and thanked the siblings who attended, showing that she still wants to control others. Passive-aggressive behavior can be hard to spot, but it's obvious here because she used guilt and shame disguised as praise and gratitude. In Danielle's mind, everyone should have been there. Since they weren't, she subtly expressed her anger and judgment. She tried to scold, guilt, or shame those who dared to defy her perception of good behavior.

Everyone has the God-given right to decide whether to attend a funeral without fearing judgment from others. Jesus didn't teach that attending funerals is required. He knew that the person's spirit was no longer present and that, at the moment of death, the spirit had already returned to our Father in heaven.

In Luke 9:60, Jesus said, "Let the dead bury their own dead, but you go and proclaim the kingdom of God." Jesus views unloving people as spiritually dead. Instead of spending time with such people, we can better use our time teaching others about our Father's love and how to attain eternal life.

I raised the stakes by asking them to help Darcy with food and money, and in doing so, I earned myself strike seven. How dare I? Their giving is private. Their church teaches them not to let their left hand see what their right hand is giving. Many use this as an excuse, so that no one will know if they give nothing. Some now see me as bossy. They don't like being asked by their Gentile sister to open their pocketbooks.

There's no doubt in my mind that I got strike eight when I quoted another Bible verse, as they look down their noses at

Gentiles who quote Bible verses. To them, those who don't share their beliefs don't have God's only truth and are Gentiles destined for hell. If we mention Bible verses to them, in their eyes, we're just spouting a false religion. That causes daggers to shoot out of their eyes and makes their ears slam shut.

I admit I used the Bible verse about helping others to guilt-trip them. I included the verse because only a few people responded to help with the food drive. Darcy mentioned on the phone that the cards and money she received at the funeral were all from her side of the family. She had received no financial help from Jerry's side. I wanted to remind them how Poppa feels about that. I thought they needed a reminder that if we have God in us, and if we are able, we are to show love and compassion to others when they are in need.

Their thoughts and prayers for Darcy were enough. Did they think God would drop food and enormous sums of money from the sky for her? In their minds, God was going to take care of her without insurance or their help. He will cover her hospital and burial expenses.

I'll call their bluff. People who only offer their fluffy thoughts and prayers, with no action, if they have the means, have shut up their bowels of compassion; and God is not in them.

If their preacher had been the one organizing a food drive for Darcy, I'm sure they would have been in their kitchen with food flying everywhere. They would look pious to their "man of God." Their preacher would never do a food drive for someone who didn't attend his church. Don't ya know? Those Gentiles don't deserve help.

Oops! Strike nine. Looking back, they don't believe in life insurance. Mom has a very negative view of it. A few years ago, I asked Mom, who is getting older, if I could get her a small burial life insurance policy to cover her funeral costs. She rejected the idea in a harsh, derogatory voice and acted as if I had just asked her to eat worms. For them, buying life insurance is a grave sin. If they buy it, it shows they don't trust God to care for them.

I stopped counting my strikes. Every time I say something to them, it counts as a strike. Any mention of the Bible or God is worth 100 strikes. If I had a dollar for every strike, I would be rich.

Susan wished I could have heard her preacher's sermon at the funeral. She wanted me to hear his message, hoping it would enlighten me about my unworthiness of God's love. The preacher's main point was to urge everyone to prepare their souls today because no one has the promise of tomorrow. Don't roll the dice on today, as you could die at any moment. Yes, Susan. Prepare today. Repent of your unloving behavior so that when you die, you can face our Heavenly Father without shame for how you've treated others. Father is the one who holds all the cards. He knows all your judgments, criticisms, gossip, and backbiting toward others. You're right — tomorrow could be your last day. Have you been a good girl or a bad girl?

I'm prepared to meet Poppa, Susan. My deepest desire is to live my life for Him, and I long to be with Him forever. I don't believe in John Calvin's "predestination-only" theory, which claims there's nothing anyone can do to be saved. However, your preacher is coming around to Jesus' true teachings, especially with his message to prepare today.

Yes, Susan, he's correct in saying there's something you can do. Your preacher wouldn't tell you to prepare if it were impossible, right? Or will his next Sunday sermon flip-flop back to his "predestination-only" teaching that there's nothing anyone can do to be saved? Shucks, one of these days he might hit the jackpot! Can't you see? These are two extreme opposites. Anyone who teaches or believes both is a hypocrite.

My hope for you, Susan, is that Father will open His Word to you so you can see how loving, kind, gentle, patient, understanding, and compassionate He is. I hope you realize how much He loves all His children and wants us all to love Him in return. And yes, your preacher is right; our Poppa says to prepare today.

When my brother Pete died, I heard the same hypocrisy at his funeral. Once is enough for me. Twenty years ago, Pete died in a snowmobile accident. He was in his mid-twenties and still quite the party boy. He and his friends had been drinking and riding on the snow. Pete was going 120 mph when his snowmobile hit the ice. He couldn't turn. He smacked right into a telephone pole and died instantly.

Peggy was there when I arrived at Mom's house. She had already taken out her deviled eggs, was stirring the pot, and was fussing about wanting Pete's leather jacket. She said she was his favorite sister, and he would have wanted her to have it. Peggy became upset because Mom's church didn't allow flowers either at the church or by the casket at the funeral home. The preacher said flowers distracted people from hearing his message. All the flowers had to stay at the back.

I agreed we should be able to place flowers on our brother's casket. We bought a casket spray of flowers, against Mom's wishes, and a flower wreath for the pole that he had hit. The preacher had the casket flowers removed before he preached his private family sermon at the funeral home.

During the main church service, he said, "It's too late for Pete, but it's not too late for you." My jaw dropped to the floor when he condemned Pete to hell with this one little innuendo. Why would he say it was too late for Pete to be saved? Did God whisper that in his ear? It's not too late for the congregation to be saved? It's not too late for what exactly? Is there something they can do to be saved? If yes, it would be helpful if you told them how to attain salvation!

I know their church teaches predestination only and no free will. He preaches that their destiny is set in stone and that they cannot choose salvation. What exactly does he want them to do before it's too late? Some of these preachers are such hypocrites. On the one hand, they say people have no free will to choose salvation; then you hear them say such harebrained things as this. You just gotta shake your head and walk away. Just walk away!

They teach that everyone is a worthless piece of garbage and unworthy of our Poppa's love. But that's not true! Our Heavenly Father loves each of us so much that He entered a flesh body to pay the death penalty for anyone who loves Him and follows His commandments.

They don't believe that everyone can choose to ask Jesus into their heart and life. They reject the idea that Jesus died on the cross for whosoever loves Him. Susan refused to see that I am prepared to die. However, in her mind, I am not ready because I am not a member of her church. Don't ya know? They are the only people who have a chance of entering heaven. To Susan, I am a fake Christian because I don't attend her church, and I display confident joy about going to heaven.

Most of them do not go beyond feeling sorrow for their sins to accepting Jesus' gift of salvation. They believe there is nothing they can do to be saved. They never progress to becoming servants for Him. John Calvin told them that God predestined their final destination — heaven or hell — before He even created the earth. He portrayed that if they are among God's elect people — by the luck of the draw — then God will let them know. He will strike their hearts with a powerful, shocking, reverberating conviction of their sins. They will cry and hardly ever stop.

Sadie believes that a saved person who comes to fruition will enter a complete mental state of total depravity. They will realize they are worthless sinners and will remain in a state of guilt, shame, and self-hatred for the rest of their lives.

Sadie believes I'm being frivolous for spouting off religious scripture, expressing love for our Heavenly Father, and discussing how Jesus said we should behave and treat others. She believes that Gentiles never fall into complete depravity of mind. Her church teaches that God's predestined elect are only members of their church. To her, all other churches that don't teach Calvin's predestination-only doctrine are false. They are religions that will never come to fruition.

Sadie looks down her nose with extreme judgment toward anyone who talks about having a relationship with and loving our Poppa. She's critical of anyone who expresses spiritual happiness and confidence about their afterlife in heaven. Sadie judges spiritually happy people as having a religion that doesn't come to fruition. She says that we can't choose to love our Poppa. Her church teaches her to be terrified of God.

The correct definition of fruition is to reach fulfillment, the point at which a plan or project becomes realized, becomes ripe, and produces fruit.

Matthew 7:16 says, "Ye shall know them by their fruits." Fruits symbolize our actions and behavior. A good tree will show loving actions, while a corrupt tree will display unloving actions. The fruit our Father wants us to produce is love for Him, ourselves, and others.

Sadie's church doesn't teach her how to come to fruition or how to become ripe and bear fruit. John Calvin has stolen from her the core teachings of Jesus. His theft included self-reflection, remorse, apology, forgiveness, loving actions, gratitude for forgiveness, love for our Father, and becoming a servant to love and teach others about His path of love.

Many pretend Christians don't show loving fruit. They never become servants of our Heavenly Father. If someone claims to be a Christian and exhibits unloving behavior, their religion has never come to fruition. The die is cast. A good tree can't produce rotten fruit; an evil tree can't produce good fruit.

Sadie doesn't realize that it is she who has a religion that produces no good fruit. She bears rotten fruit because she believes she can't choose to love our Heavenly Poppa. Another reason she bears evil fruit is that her church teaches she can't love herself. She doesn't understand the difference between vain, conceited, ego-trip self-love and the essential, innate, God-given, healthy emotional love and self-protection.

Jesus taught us to love each other as we love ourselves. Sadie suppresses love toward herself. When she hears someone talk about the importance of self-love or if someone says they love themselves, she judges that person as "a foot too high," or as thinking too highly of themselves, and labels them a narcissist.

"Master, which is the great commandment in the law? Jesus said unto him, Thou shalt love the Lord thy God with all thy heart, and with all thy soul, and with all thy mind. This is the first and great commandment. And the second is like unto it, Thou shalt love thy neighbour as thyself. On these two commandments hang all the law and the prophets" (Mt 22:36-40).

John Calvin removed the two main commandments from the Bible. He taught that our Father is an angry, wrathful, judgmental, critical, and punishing God. This belief influences how many of my family members treat others. Their belief that God hates them and their self-hatred are the reasons they show such evil behavior toward their neighbors. They believe God gives them evil fruit, so they give themselves evil fruit as well. All they have within themselves is evil fruit to give to others.

We'll never have genuine love for others until we realize that our Father loves us. Once we understand this, we'll love Him in return. When we feel deserving, we'll love ourselves the same way He loves us. After that, we can let that love flow outward to others, knowing Poppa loves them too.

Sadie believes that I'm not saved because I don't meet her mistaken definition of fruition. She judges me as unsaved because I love myself and see myself as valued, rather than worthless. I carry a joyful confidence that I will go to heaven when I die. Sadie is wrong in her belief that a saved person won't love themselves. She also thinks they won't have a happy confidence about their afterlife in heaven. She believes they will always cry and feel sad. They will present themselves as humble and cowering.

Sadie said that I'm "a foot too high" to even speak about God. In her mind, only her preacher, elders, and deacons are the servants of God. With cruelty, she tried to sweeten the pot. She said, "He that heareth, let him understand." Sadie was using Bible code with her special church besties. She was quoting Jesus' words all the while being cruel, which is the ultimate show of her religious hierarchy and hypocrisy.

Sadie went into full demon mode and became more abusive toward me when I asked her to stop acting vicious toward me. She had to dig up mud from 12 years ago to throw at me, doing whatever it took to turn the attention away from her behavior. She didn't want to be asked to stop. When you confront and call out an abusive person's behavior, be ready for them to pull out their stack of chips. They'll bring up things from years ago to make accusations against you. With cruelty, they try to bring you down to the size they want you to be.

Sadie went into full demon mode because I said that I am the apple of our Heavenly Father's eye. I'm surprised she didn't say I was now 3 feet too high. Sadie sees me as an unholy, free-willed Gentile destined for hell. Because — like all of Poppa's servants — I'm happy and speak confidently about my relationship with Him.

Sadie had the cards stacked against me because she was part of a secret group message with some of my other abusive siblings. Birds of a feather flock together and get their abuse juice from each other. Sadie told me — the non-abuser — that I need to get my head checked. She was implying I don't have a full deck upstairs, and she truly believes this. She doesn't see that her behavior is abusive. It was she who was cruel. Yet she told me I'm the one who is a few cards short of a deck.

The reason she said that I have lost my marbles is that she doesn't enjoy being called out for her cruel and abusive behavior. She made it seem like I have a problem and need help. Abusive people often gaslight others, and it's important to recognize their tactics and respond with facts.

Sadie telling me to get a day job was her looking down her nose at me. She was being critical and judgmental toward me because I work the overnight shift. If I had been working the hours she considers normal, then I wouldn't be sending daytime text messages asking her to stop abusing me. She was looking for anything to make me feel less valuable than her. She tried to divert the conversation to be about me so I would stop calling her out on her cruel and abusive behavior.

Sadie overplayed her hand when she brought up my personal grievances with two other siblings from the past. She learned about these through gossip. I'm glad she mentioned them, though, because it gave me a chance to shed light on the darkness. She thought she was being hurtful to me. Instead, I appreciated the opportunity to lay these other hurtful experiences on the table.

Some family members got lost in the shuffle and didn't join the group message. They wanted nothing to do with the cruel family members. Others chimed in a little, sharing a bit of love or a bit of hate, depending on their personalities. Some had a chip on their shoulder. They stated facts only to avoid engaging with people they didn't like.

Nobody in my family stood up for me. I realized that 2000 years ago, nobody in the crowd stood up for Jesus either as the murderers chanted, "Crucify Him! Crucify Him!" They feared the vicious, cruel, and unloving religious scribes and Pharisees. They worried the Pharisees would turn on them, excommunicate them from the church, or put them to death. I'm sure the ones who didn't dare stand up for me feared that Sadie, Peggy, Danielle, Jolene, and Susan would turn their evil fruit toward them and crucify them as well.

Love for our Poppa is unfamiliar to my family. They don't tell Father that they love Him, even though that's what He desires most from us. Jesus' teachings about love and loving behavior were also unfamiliar in His day. Many ordinary people loved Jesus and His teachings, but their fear of the vicious religious leaders kept many from standing up for Him.

I'm no longer afraid of vicious, cruel, and hurtful people. The worst that can happen is they get blotted out on Judgment Day. On that day, those with loving hearts will have the trump card. I'm Poppa's servant. I know they are His children, and He loves them very much. He doesn't want to blot out any of His children. It will make Father very sad. He will experience tremendous heartache when He has to cast His unloving children into the lake of fire. This isn't like us discarding a bad egg or a rotten tomato. Instead, Father will have to destroy His unloving children who refuse to love Him and His other children.

With my family, you can teach about love until you're blue in the face. They won't hear you. Their ears are closed. They are behind the eight ball. Their brainwashing is strong. They believe that nobody deserves Poppa's love. This is such an abusive teaching. Just imagine you have a baby, and then you hate, neglect, kick, hit, yell at it, and throw it into the fireplace to burn. All the while, you watch as it screams in pain and torment. That is literally what their church portrays to them. They don't believe our Father loves all His children. Every baby deserves their parents' love and affection. All normal human parents love their babies very much. Our Poppa is supernatural, so instead, He has super-duper love for all of us, His children.

If Sadie believed that our Father loves us, then she would know how to love and share it with others. Sadie's church depicts a hellfire, damnation, wrathful, angry, and hateful

God. As we see with Sadie, extreme religion can make people vicious. She has placed her bets in a burning house!

During this family group chat, I received a personal message from Anna saying she had heard — through gossip, of course — that Darcy has a gambling addiction, so be careful when sending her money. I told Anna I had already sent it and would leave it in Father's hands. I told her we can't leave Darcy and nine children out on the street.

A week after the family chat had folded, I spoke with Darcy on the phone. She told me she had received no cards or money from any of the family members. I told Darcy that they weren't sending money because they believed she would gamble it.

This devastated Darcy. She said all she did was go with Ben's wife to some random bingo nights. Darcy, in past times, during innocent conversations, was naïve and mentioned this to one of them. Playing some bingo landed her as an unworthy sinner.

My heart breaks for Darcy, and it also breaks for my cruel siblings, who think that such hateful behavior is acceptable. Of course, when they spread their hateful gossip about Darcy, they didn't mention that it was only a few occasional bingo games. They judged Darcy to be unworthy of their help because they believed she was a gambling sinner destined for hell.

I'm glad we're not living in their ancestors' era, when the hangings took place during the Salem Witch Trials. They would have hanged Darcy from a tree long ago for her occasional playing of the Devil's bingo game. However, in their eyes, simply because she didn't attend their church, they deemed her unworthy of their help. Their bingo card is filling up fast as they stack up their chips of unloving behavior.

Play your cards close to your chest when sharing personal information with my family. In their hearts, they are always judging those around them. Their house of cards will come crashing down when Jesus returns. Their embarrassment and shame for all the bad hands they've dealt others will make them wish the mountains would fall on them. They'll desire death but won't find it. When Jesus arrives, all unloving people will be on their knees. They will be holding the dead man's hand.

Time, distance, work, having our own families, finances, religious beliefs, religious hierarchy, judgments, condescending gossip, backbiting, lack of love, childhood abuse, childhood neglect, and personal traumas have torn our family apart.

It's unlikely there will ever be a day when our family stops hurting each other. Many of them have become addicted to hate, criticism, and judging. They don't want to choose love. I hope that one day we can all come together and be a loving family. Father, our Lord and Savior, Jesus, is the only King who can put Humpty Dumpty back together again.

You can bet your bottom dollar that I don't want to be included in any future family group messages that include hateful people. There's no need to notify me when these cruel people pass away. Cruel people are spiritually dead; they are not my spiritual family.

People like that don't bring joy and happiness to my life. Only loving people are my family. They are the only ones who can spend eternity in heaven. Jesus said in Matthew 12:50, "Whosoever shall do the will of my Father which is in heaven, the same is my brother, and sister, and mother." Father's will is that we love one another. Cruel people are not my brother, sister, or mother. They won't enter the Pearly Gates.

Anyone or any church that teaches and brainwashes others into believing they aren't worthy of Father's love and that they should not love themselves is committing severe abuse. This harmful and false teaching is nothing less than pure, raw abuse to all the children born into this passed-down, generational belief system. It causes these children to suffer a lifetime of deep trauma, making them always feel less than others, insecure, and unworthy of love. They develop an inability to live a normal life or grow into happy, confident, loving adults. Deluded, brainwashed adults steal this essential love — one of our most basic human needs — from them. These adults, when they were children, also had this same love ripped away from them.

These innocent babies who are born into abusive religious belief systems have no chance against the intense brainwashing they receive from the moment of birth. Anyone — whether at home, church, or school — who makes little children believe they aren't worthy of our Poppa's love and teaches them that loving themselves is a sin should be charged with abuse. The damage caused to these children has tragic, lifelong consequences, leaving them with trauma and a persistent feeling of unworthiness.

The path to spiritual happiness begins with the understanding that love is the complete answer to the whole meaning of life. We can start this journey of love by engaging in deep, honest self-reflection. Who are we? Where did we come from? How did we arrive here? This reflection helps us find our purpose in life. We should make introspection a lifelong friend.

Examine all past actions to determine which are loving and which are hurtful. We can shove our findings under the rug or embrace love. Allowing tears to flow helps us feel regret for our mistakes. It's important to give sincere apologies to those we have hurt, including ourselves. We should analyze which behaviors are not loving and then change them. Do we want to love or hurt others?

We receive forgiveness when we accept responsibility for our actions and apologize. This feels good. A burden lifts from our chests. As we recognize, focus on, analyze, and listen to these pre-programmed feelings of love within ourselves, we then want to know who created us this way. We seek the creator of this incredible love.

When we consistently follow the law of love within us, we realize that our Creator must also be loving. We see that He is our Father, and He loves us very much. As we talk to Him, we ask for His forgiveness for our past mistakes and unloving actions. We understand that we need help on our journey of love. He will come into our lives to guide us. Just as everyone else forgives us when we apologize, our Father will also forgive us. Just like all wonderful moms and dads do when their children say they're sorry.

Knowing that He's an amazing Poppa, we feel deep gratitude for His forgiveness. We love Him in return. Then we share His forgiveness, love, and compassion with others. We trim our wick daily to keep our candle of love burning brightly for everyone around us. Setting out on our path of love, we aim to become ripe and to bear good fruit.

We now understand that Poppa wishes all His children to engage in deep introspection. He desires everyone to feel remorse and to apologize. He hopes that all of His children will choose only loving actions.

Now, we let our Father's love fill our hearts, souls, and minds. In desiring to serve Him, we radiate His love, forgiveness, and compassion toward others. We teach as many people as possible about His beautiful heavenly realm. We become in tune with what Poppa wants. He desires all His children to choose His beautiful path of love — to live together forever in heavenly bliss.

I forgive my family in my heart. We grew up in an extremely abusive home. They haven't yet made it through to the other side of the waterfall. I hope that one day they can find peace, joy, love, and happiness. I can't wait for them to join me as we dig through the pot of gold at the end of the rainbow. Considering all we went through and all they are still enduring, I have great compassion for them. What I shared with you is just a sliver of the aftereffects of the massive trauma we all suffered as kids. You can read about our old, scary chicken farm and how lucky we all are to be alive in my other book, "Scrambled Eggs, Walking on Shells." I'll see you there.

www.ingramcontent.com/pod-product-compliance
Lightning Source LLC
LaVergne TN
LVHW010925110826
845149LV00013B/2479

* 9 7 9 8 9 9 4 6 2 0 0 7 6 *